HOW I F*CKING DID IT

From Moving Elves to Making Over Six-Figures on the Internet and You Can Too

JEN MANN

Throat Punch Media, LLC

Copyright 2019 by Throat Punch Media, LLC

All rights reserved.

No part of this story may be used, reproduced, or transmitted in any matter whatsoever, including but not limited to electronic or mechanical means, photocopying, recording, or by any information storage and retrieval system without written permission in writing from the author, except in the case of brief quotations embodied in the critical articles and reviews.

Dedicated to the dreamers. I'm totally disorganized, a procrastinator, and an absolute pain in the ass. If I can do this, anyone can!

Contents

Timeline	vii
Introduction	ix
1. So You Wanna Be A Writer? Quit Talking About It And Do It Already	1
2. I Said Quit Talking And Start Doing	9
3. The Little Bastard That Changed My Life	25
4. F*Ck Fear	35
5. Make Some Rules	41
6. Cool Story, Jen, But How Do I Go Viral?	49
7. Get To Work	55
8. Always Be Building	65
9. Just Publish Your Book	73
10. Make Some Friends	85
11. Get Yourself a Hype Man	99
12. Let's Write A Book Proposal	113
13. I Think It Might Be Easier To Find A Spouse Than An Agent	125
14. Let's Make Some Money	141
15. Publish An Anthology	153
16. Put On Some Pants And Leave The House	163
17. Don't Forget Why You Do This	173
Acknowledgments	177
A Note From Jen	179
Follow Jen	181
Other Books Available	183

Timeline

Fall 2006 – Hubs lost his job and we started selling real estate together.

April 2011 – I started my blog People I Want to Punch in the Throat.

December 2011 – I wrote a blog post called "Overachieving Elf on the Shelf Mommies."

December 2011 – That post went viral.

December 2011 – Started blogging five days a week.

October 2012 – Self-published *Spending the Holidays with People I Want to Punch in the Throat*.

February 2013 – Self-published *I Just Want to Pee Alone*.

February 2013 – Signed with my first publishing agent.

March 2013 – Signed a two-book deal with Penguin Random House.

March 2014 – Self-published *I Just Want to Be Alone*.

September 2014 – *People I Want to Punch in the Throat: Competitive Crafters, Drop-off Despots, and Other Suburban Scourges* is published by Penguin Random House.

March 2015 – Self-published *I STILL Just Want to Pee Alone*.

Timeline

April 2015 – Self-published *Just a Few People I Want to Punch in the Throat: Volume One*.

May 2015 – Self-published *Just a Few People I Want to Punch in the Throat: Volume Two*.

June 2015 – Self-published *Just a Few People I Want to Punch in the Throat: Volume Three*.

August 2015 – Self-published *Just a Few People I Want to Punch in the Throat: Volume Four*.

October 2015 – *Spending the Holidays with People I Want to Punch in the Throat: Yuletide Yahoos, Ho-Ho-Humblebraggers, and Other Seasonal Scourges* is published by Penguin Random House.

February 2016 – Self-published *Just a Few People I Want to Punch in the Throat: Volume Five*.

May 2016 – Self-published *I Just Want to Be Perfect*.

March 2017 – Self-published *Just a Few People I Want to Punch in the Throat: Volume Six*.

April 2017 – Self-published *My Lame Life: Queen of the Misfits*.

May 2017 – Self-published *But Did You Die?*

June 2017 – Self-published *Working with People I Want to Punch in the Throat: Cantankerous Clients, Micromanaging Minions, and Other Supercilious Scourges*.

September 2018 – Self-published *You Do You!*

December 2018 – Self-published *Just a Few People I Want to Punch in the Throat: Volumes One – Six*.

March 2019 – Self-published *How I F*cking Did It: From Moving Elves to Making Over Six-Figures on the Internet and You Can Too*.

Introduction

WAIT. I'M SORRY, WHO THE HELL ARE YOU, JEN?

Hi there, I'm Jen Mann. I'm a middle-aged, minivan-driving mama who uses the F-bomb like a comma and despises wearing pants. I'm also the award-winning blogger behind the popular website People I Want to Punch in the Throat and the *New York Times* bestselling author of several hilarious books, including *People I Want to Punch in the Throat: Competitive Crafters, Drop-off Despots, and Other Suburban Scourges* and *I Just Want to Pee Alone*.

In 2011 I was a brand-new blogger with seventy subscribers and absolutely no social media platform when I wrote a blog post called "Overachieving Elf on the Shelf Mommies." That blog post was read by over one million people in twenty-four hours and single-handedly launched a career I'd only ever dreamed about. I took that stroke of luck and got to work. Since then I've gone from starting a blog to writing and publishing over fourteen titles and six hundred blog posts, all while growing my social media following to more than one million people. I've also helped dozens of writers publish their work and find success. All this to say, I'm kind of a big deal at my mom's Bunko club, so surely you've heard of me.

Wait. You don't know who I am? You're just sitting in a carpool line surfing on your phone or in your cubicle at lunchtime with your turkey sandwich looking for something to inspire you to get your ass in gear and you've never heard of me? (That sort of hurts my giant ego, but I understand.) Well, let's get you caught up, shall we?

As I said before, I'm Jen. Unless you're talking about me pre-1990, then I'm Jenni. Notice it's not "Jennifer." My parents went wild and put their own flavor on a classic by putting an adorable "i" on the end, showing how unique they are and thereby killing all possibility of me becoming a heart surgeon. When you have a name that ends in an adorable "i" that can only be written with a heart for a dot, it guarantees you'll end up either on the pole or on the keyboard. Luckily, I chose the keyboard.

I have two kids: Gomer and Adolpha (both teenagers at the writing of this book). Before you have a hissy fit and sit down to write me a nasty letter about my children's horrible names, just stop. *Of course* those aren't their real names. Their real names are actually worse, but I can't take the ridicule, so I just made up what I consider to be horrific names for them in everything I write.

I'm married to Ebeneezer, but I usually call him The Hubs. You can call him The Hubs too. Everyone does. He's a cheap bastard who can be a tad antisocial, but he treats me like gold, so he's my lobster.

I've lived in Iowa, New Jersey, Illinois, Kansas, and New York. I currently live in Kansas. It doesn't blow as much as you'd think it would. I don't live on a farm or anything like that. I live in a suburb with McMansions and

Introduction

award-winning schools. It's like its own circle of hell, but with Targets and Starbucks on every corner.

So, what do you think? Are you still thinking about buying this book? What was it exactly that drew you in? The cover? The title? A review you read somewhere? Fantastic! I'm so happy.

But. Before you spend your hard-earned cash on this book and then hate it and leave me a shitty review, let's have a quick chat about what to expect. You did see on the cover where it says *How I F*cking Did It*, right? I'm a bit abrasive. I'm not going to blow rainbows and sunshine up your ass. While this is a beneficial and entertaining book, it is not for everyone. Yes, I'm going to give you a fuck-ton of advice, but it's not going to be sugarcoated or tied up with an *ah-dor-able* bow to make it go down easier. I've grown my little empire, and I've made well over six figures writing on the internet, and I've learned some shit I will share with you. This book is half inspiration, half how-to, and half motivation. Wait, that's too many halves, isn't it? Eh, who cares? I'm a writer, not a mathematician. Basically, I'm going to tell you what I did right (and what I did wrong) and then I'm going to give you a very friendly, non-sexual virtual slap on the ass and tell you to get to work, because if I can do this, you definitely can too!

Are you still in? Great. Let's get to work.

1

So You Wanna Be A Writer? Quit Talking About It And Do It Already

"I hate writing, I love having written."

Dorothy Parker

When I tell people I'm a full-time writer, the most common reactions I get are:

"Oh, I've been thinking about doing that, but it seems like a lot of work." *I won't lie to you. It is.*

"Maybe I'll do that in a few years when I have some time." *Yeah, that's not a good plan. Trust me. You'll never have the time unless you make the time.*

"How do you know what to write about?" *If you don't know, I can't tell you.*

"Can you even make money doing that?" *You bet.*

I get it. I really do. Because I didn't start writing professionally until I was in my late thirties even though I wanted to be a writer since I was five years old. When I was five years old I discovered that writing books was a real job.

"You mean people get paid to do this?" I asked, looking up from my favorite book.

My mother nodded. "Well, of course, Jenni. No one works for free," she said.

"But I mean, it's a *job* to write the books I read?" I asked.

"Yes, the person is called an author."

Author. I rolled the word over in my brain and smiled with delight. "I want to be an *author*," I said, trying the word out loud.

My mother indulged me with a small laugh and a pat on the head. "Yes, yes," she said. "You can be an author."

Little did I know then but I could have said I wanted to be a lion tamer or an astronaut or president of the United States and she would have behaved the same exact way. Because that's what mothers do. Mothers enable our dreams when we're small. They want us to believe we can achieve anything we set our hearts to. They're not in the business of dream-crushing, at least not when you're five.

I'm doing it right now to my own kids. I tell my kids to reach for the stars and try for those dreams, but deep down inside, I'm like, *Shit, I have no idea how Adolpha is going to become a designer of high-end clothing for dogs!* Because I don't know anyone who does that for a living. I have no connections or experience in that world. The Hubs and I buy all our clothes from Sam's Club and Target; we wouldn't know high-end fashion if it hit us in the face. And we don't even own a dog! But we nod encouragingly and tell Adolpha to go for it! We figure she can study design and fashion and somehow harness the power of the internet and achieve those dreams. Maybe?? Probably?? Definitely!!

But when I was five years old, the internet and the opportunities it affords to creative people didn't exist yet. And self-publishing was an expensive way to feed your ego.

I was a kid in suburban Iowa and all the publishing was done in New York City. Those giant publishing houses felt like guarded and secretive clubs you had to be invited to join, and I had no idea how to get an invitation. I didn't know any writers, so I grew up believing they were solitary, depressed people who dressed in black and worked like hermits in tiny cold-water flats in Brooklyn and sent off their pages via courier to their agents who would weep and say, "Yes! This will be the greatest work of your life!" (I can say I wasn't that far off from my reality. I do wear all black, I'm more pissed off than depressed, and I hate to leave my house. Now, if I could just write the greatest work of my life...)

Over the years I filled countless notebooks with my scribbles. I jotted down the beginnings of hundreds of stories, I made up dialogue when I was in the shower, and I dreamed up magical realms each night while I waited for sleep to come. I escaped from my (boring) real life into books as much as possible.

When I was in high school I found an English teacher who believed in my talent and encouraged me to write. Mr. Williams was always very supportive, and he always worked hard to help push me out of my comfort zone. He was the first person (outside of my parents) who liked what I wrote and demanded to see more. He was also the first person who wasn't related to me who made me think maybe a career as a writer wasn't a stupid, unattainable pipe dream. Up until that point, whenever any adult would ask me what I wanted to do with my life I'd reply, "Be an author." They'd laugh and say, "Good luck with that!" But not Mr. Williams.

When it came time to apply for college Mr. Williams asked me what I was going to study. "Education, probably," I mumbled.

"What? Why?" he asked, shaking his head.

Here's the thing, my parents believed in me, they did, but they also understood how hard it is to succeed as a writer. They didn't want me living in their basement working on my Great American Novel for the rest of my life. They had suggested I get a teaching degree as "a backup" in case that whole *New York Times* bestselling author thing didn't work out.

"If you're a teacher, you can always write over the summers," my mom had said helpfully.

"You'll need benefits," my dad had said wisely.

"My parents think I need a 'real' job and writing isn't a real job," I said. "They want me to teach."

"Hmm," Mr. Williams said, frowning. "I don't know about that."

"Why not?" I asked.

"Well, I just can't see you as a teacher. You hate school now. Can you imagine working here?"

I grimaced. "Not really," I said. "But my dad says I need benefits. Teachers get benefits."

"Barely," Mr. Williams quipped. "Look, I'm not going to argue with your parents, but I think you should go for it. You should major in creative writing and you should try to make it. You're one of my most talented students. You can do it, Jenni!"

I was pleased Mr. Williams believed in me, but I didn't believe a word he said. I was sure he was projecting his own regrets onto me. He was in his early thirties and his first child had been born that year, tying him down even tighter to his job. He seemed so old to me. In my seventeen-year-old mind, I thought you had to find success as a writer by twenty-five or else the opportunity was lost. I have no idea where that number came from. I'd probably read an article somewhere about the average age of first-time authors or something stupid like that.

I went home that day and really thought about what he'd said. My parents had been the ones feeding my ego for the last twelve years, telling me I could do anything (except live in their basement forever) and now that I believed them and I was ready to do it, they were changing their minds!

I broached the subject with them again. It didn't go as well as my conversation with Mr. Williams.

"What will you do for money?" Dad asked. "How will you support yourself as a writer? What sort of jobs are there for writers?"

I didn't have an answer because I really didn't know ways writers could support themselves. If my novels didn't sell, what was my backup plan, really? Instead of researching and learning, I just gave up. Giving up on writing was something I did a lot, because in those days I was a talker. I was always *going* to write a book. I just needed the perfect conditions. I needed the right inspiration or characters to jump into my brain. I needed perfect silence. I needed a certain pen or pencil or notebook. I needed more time. Instead of starting, I kept talking, and researching, and dreaming, and talking some more. I should have just put my butt in a chair and gotten to work back then. Can you imagine what I would have accomplished by now if I had?

But I didn't. Instead, I caved and agreed to be a teacher.

I went down that path for exactly two weeks.

I enrolled in college as an elementary education major. I'd been told by my advisor that was the best route. She explained that elementary education was great, because it was an easy, low-stress job with little responsibility and lots of free time. And it was absolutely perfect for women who wanted a family. I had not said a thing about wanting a low-stress job or a family, but I signed up anyway. Now that I've had two children go through elementary school and I've befriended tons of elementary school teachers, I'd like to go back and punch that woman in the throat, because she obviously had no clue what she was talking about. Teaching is a ridiculously hard and time-consuming job. Oh, and Mr. Williams was so right: I didn't like kids. At all.

I think I was in some sort of class learning how to communicate with gifted students or something, but I do remember thinking, *This is horseshit. I do not want to do this. I don't know what I'll do for money, but I know I will be a horrible teacher. I don't like school or kids. Why in the world would I choose this for my occupation?* I figured as much as they threatened, my parents would really never let me end up homeless, so I walked out of class and went straight to the registrar's office and declared myself a creative writing major.

I didn't tell my parents. I decided it was a conversation best had in person when I returned home for Thanksgiving. I didn't think my parents would flip out in front of the grandparents, so I waited until everyone was around the dinner table and then I did the whole, "I changed my major to creative writing, please pass the mashed potatoes!" (Hey, it could have been worse, at least I didn't tell them I was pregnant.)

There was a bit of chaos, but I'd done my research and I was better prepared this time when my parents peppered me with questions about my future earnings potential. "I've already landed a job writing for the alumni magazine. I'll graduate with experience and I'm earning money from writing! [It wasn't even enough to pay for my text books, but that wasn't the point.] I can be a copywriter or work in public relations," I said. "I can be a technical writer. Who knows? There are tons of writing jobs out there! Everything you read has to be written by someone. I'll be that someone!" I trotted out these office jobs with ease, but deep down I envisioned myself in my jammies, writing books. I didn't know how or when I'd do it, but I knew that was the ultimate goal.

Little did I know, it would take another fifteen years to get there.

How You Can F*cking Do It:

- Quit talking and start doing.
- Believe in yourself.
- Write what you want to write.
- Don't worry about what other people will think.

2

I Said Quit Talking And Start Doing

"If I waited for perfection, I'd never write."

Margaret Atwood

It was the fall of 2006 and I was a work-at-home mom with a toddler and a baby due any day when my husband, Ebeneezer, called to tell me his entire department had been laid off and he was headed home.

"But...but..." I stuttered, clamping my legs shut and willing the baby inside me not to drop to the floor, because I no longer had insurance to cover her birth. "You're the one who makes all the money. You're the one with the benefits and the company car! And the 401(k)!"

I was a fairly successful Realtor, but this pregnancy had been rough on me, and I hadn't been putting as much effort into my business as I had in the past. I'd been coasting because the Hubs had a good job and we didn't need my income to live on, just to pay some bills here and there or go on vacation.

"It's okay, Jen," Ebeneezer assured me. "I have a plan."

Now, the thing you need to understand about my husband is he *always* has a plan. And sometimes his plans are downright genius and sometimes his plans are absolute trash. I wasn't sure which kind of plan this one was going to be.

"What kind of plan?" I whimpered, looking around the house we'd bought the year before. It was definitely a two-income house, and I wasn't sure if I could swing more than the electric bill on my own.

"I will come to work for you!" Ebeneezer announced proudly.

"Wait. What?" I felt the baby drop even lower. "That's a terrible idea!" I fumbled for a chair and sat down heavily.

"Why?" he asked. "You're exhausted, you've got a baby due any day now, and you need help. You've been looking to hire someone to help you with your client load. You won't be able to do as much once the baby comes. You need an employee. I'm better than an employee. I can be your *partner*."

I immediately imagined my life as a single mother, because married people don't work together. It's just not done. I loved Ebeneezer, but I didn't like him enough to work with him every single day. And partners? Was he kidding? This was my business! It wasn't much, but it was mine! These were my clients! I'd worked hard to cultivate those relationships and to earn their trust, and now he thought he could just roll in and make himself a partner?

Yes, I needed some help, but not that much. The last time I had a baby, I was back at work with two-week-old Gomer strapped to my chest closing deals and making shit happen. This pregnancy had slowed me down a bit, but once Adolpha was out, I would bounce back quickly and she would join my team too. I was Superwoman and Super Mom all rolled into one! I didn't need the Hubs micromanaging me and bossing me around, because that was what was going to happen. We're very different people. I need to complain, and he needs to fix things. I don't want to be fixed; I just want to be heard. He doesn't want to listen; he only wants to fix. I just want to vent and have him nod along and say, "Yeah, fuck that." Instead, he's all, "Well, you know, you could try..." No! No! No! Fuck that!

"We're going to get divorced," I cried.

"We won't get divorced," Ebeneezer assured me. "Because I understand you. As long as you're in charge, everything is okay. I'll be your bitch boy. I will run all the errands and deal with all the stuff you don't want to do. It will still be your team and your name on the signs and the front door. We'll be partners in life, but you will be the boss lady in the office."

I had to admit, I didn't hate the sound of "boss lady."

"I guess it could work," I said reluctantly.

"Of course it will work. No one will work as hard for you as I will."

That was true, I thought. *Ebeneezer's a worker.*

"And I have ideas, Jen! I have a vision for you! No one will care about growing your business as much as I will."

Also true, but ugh...was this really the only solution?

"I don't know ..."

He silenced me. "And you won't have to pay me."

"You're hired," I said.

AND THAT'S how the Hubs and I became co-workers. I mean, partners. Originally, the deal was we'd only do it for a few months. He'd just help me out with the business and the kids until I felt like I was ready to go back full-time and he found a "real" job. It was supposed to be temporary. We had no idea then that the country was on the brink of the Great Recession and that in a few months millions of people would be out of work and the housing market would collapse and we'd have to make our partnership permanent if we were going to survive.

Even though it was a temporary arrangement, Ebeneezer started making big changes right off the bat. He's a cheap bastard, and since we'd lost a salary, he decided we (I) needed to tighten our (my) belts. We quit paying expensive desk fees to my brokerage. Ever since Gomer was born I'd pretty much been working from home full-time anyway. There was no sense paying fees for a desk I never used, but once Ebeneezer also moved into my small basement office, all I could think about was how priceless that desk at the brokerage was. We pulled Gomer out of daycare and once Adolpha was born she never went. Ebeneezer had visions of our children playing quietly at our feet while we shared parenting and household chores equally and closed million-dollar deals.

It was a fucking nightmare.

I was miserable. No matter where I went in my house a child or my husband followed me. I'd beg to go to the store by myself and Ebeneezer would say, "You don't want to do that. We'll help you!" and then he'd pile everyone into the car so we could go together. So then I'd beg to stay home alone and he'd say we didn't really need anything from the store anyway and no one would go. I never had a moment to myself. I'd only had a roommate in college for a few years and after that I'd lived on my own until I was thirty. I am a person who NEEDS my alone time. I don't like being around people a lot, even the ones I love. Ebeneezer doesn't understand this. He's never been on his own. He moved out of his parents' basement and into a house with me. He hates to be alone, and he hates for me to be alone.

On top of my lack of "me time," working with the Hubs, raising two kids, and weathering an economic nightmare was more than I could easily bounce back from. I felt like I was failing at everything. I was not a great Realtor, I was an okayish mom, and a terrible wife. I've always been a "venter" and work was a great place to do it. The problem now was I only had one co-worker to complain to about my job and life, and he was the one I wanted to complain about!

Every night we'd go to bed and Ebeneezer would turn over and look deep into my eyes and say earnestly, "What did you do today, Jen?"

I wanted to scream, "What did I do today? YOU WERE THERE! YOU SAW WHAT I DID! YOU'RE ALWAYS THERE!"

Because we were self-employed and didn't have a steady income, we always had to think about the future. We were never not working. We'd go out for date night and all Ebeneezer wanted to talk about was my pipeline and what kind of sales goals I had for the upcoming year. I just wanted to talk about anything that wasn't business. Even the goddamn weather. I was sick of being married to my business partner. I felt like I'd lost my husband and gained an office manager.

When the recession hit later that year, it was clear that Ebeneezer and I would be full-time partners whether I liked it or not. I gave up wishing and hoping he'd find something else. I decided I needed to get on board with my new normal or else I *was* going to get divorced.

The thing is, I've never been a happy-go-lucky kind of person or a glass-is-half-full type. I've always been a bit salty and easily irritated, so when we reached the five-year mark of working together, parenting together, sleeping together, peeing together, etc., I was, of course, starting to lose my fucking mind and was super close to a full-on meltdown.

That's when Ebeneezer said to me, "We need to talk."

Uh-oh. That's never good, I thought. I felt my blood pressure rise.

"This isn't working, Jen," he said.

Shit, shit, shit. "See? I told you we'd end up divorced!" I said, pointing a finger at him. "It just took longer than I thought it would."

"What are you talking about?"

"You're the one who wanted to work together. I told you to find a real job. Your own job. You wanted to do this. I'm not to blame. This is your fault!"

The Hubs looked completely confused. "I don't want a divorce."

"You don't?"

He shook his head. "No, not at all. I think our marriage is great. It's even better now that we're working together and spending so much time together."

"You think all that time together is good?" I asked incredulously.

"Yes, you don't?"

I decided we didn't need to go down that road just yet, so I said, "What's not working then?"

"Your attitude," he said simply.

I wanted to scream, "MY ATTITUDE?" Instead I said, "Pardon me?" I like to say "pardon me" when I'm offended so people can rethink their word choice and come back with a more acceptable phrase for me.

The Hubs didn't get the hint. "Your. Attitude," he said slowly, like I really didn't hear him properly. "It's not good. You've changed. You're so angry all the time."

"I was angry when you married me," I argued. "You knew what you were getting into."

He nodded. "Yes, I get that. But you were also funny, and now you're just angry. In fact, you're angrier than ever. You're really unhappy, and I want to help you."

"Great. You should get a job. Or I should get a job. Either way, we should stop working together. It's too much. It's too much togetherness. I need some space."

"Oh, Jen. I told you I love working together. We're such a great team," he said enthusiastically. I really couldn't argue, because after five years, we had found a system that worked and because we had opposite strengths and weaknesses, we actually were a pretty decent team. But a solo vacation every now and again would have been terrific.

"No," he said. "I think we should get you some help."

I immediately felt a weight lifted off my shoulders. Finally! He understood I was drowning. "Yes, great idea," I said. "We should put the kids in daycare. We should get a nanny. And a housekeeper. And a cook."

He smiled. "Now, see? There's the funny, wisecracking girl I married!" he said.

"I wasn't making a joke," I said. "So, what are you suggesting then? I should see a doctor? Oh my god, you think I'm crazy." I glared at him. There is nothing I hate more than being called crazy. It makes me crazy. I was like, *Call me crazy one more time, Hubs. I dare you.*

"No, our insurance is terrible. We can't afford that. However, you definitely need therapy, and I have a plan!"

Remember what I said earlier about Ebeneezer's plans? I wasn't sure where he was going. "What kind of plan?"

"Well, you're a writer."

"Kinda," I said. I mean, yes, I had graduated with my degree in creative writing and I'd found several paying jobs over the years where I wrote articles, books, and speeches. I just wrote them for other people. I hadn't written anything creative since I left college. I'd had a terrible experience with a professor who shattered my confidence when he told me no one would buy a want ad I wrote. I'd let his words hold so much power over me that I'd never finished anything. I had a lot of awful half-finished books in a drawer somewhere that hadn't seen the light of day in more than a decade. I hadn't written anything new since we'd gotten married, and I'd barely read a book since Adolpha had been born. At that point most of my writing focused on overusing words like "bright and airy" and "move-in ready."

"Writing is a form of therapy," Ebeneezer said.

"Okay..."

"Blogging is writing," he said.

"Blogging?" I asked. I wasn't really sure what a blog was. The only thing I knew about blogging was my sister-in-law, Ida, had a blog where she updated everyone about her kids' lives and stuff like that. I'd read it a few times, but I didn't see the point since I had a phone and I could call her and ask about my niece and nephew. I also did not like the fact that strangers were reading about her life. "What the hell?" I'd asked her. "Do you even know these people?"

She'd shrugged. "I feel like I know a lot of them. Some of them I talk to more than you."

"That's insane."

(Cut to now and I'm like, "Some of my best friends are strangers on the internet and I'd rather hang out online with them instead of actual, real people I've known for years." I get it now. But back then I thought she was fucking nuts.)

"You should start a mommy blog," Ebeneezer said.

"A mommy blog?" I asked. "What the hell is a mommy blog?"

"I read an article about them. All the moms have one and you should too! It's a place on the internet where you can go and write about your life and your kids or your hobbies or whatever."

"Like Ida's website?"

"Yeah, but different. It would be whatever you want to talk about. It doesn't need to be just like Ida's. Ida writes what she wants to write; you'd write whatever is on your mind. You don't need to copy her or anything. The point is, it's writing and writing is therapy, so you'll feel better when you write."

"Hmm," I said skeptically.

Something you should know about me is I hate change and I hate trying new things. It takes a lot of convincing to get me to do something different. Normally I vetoed ninety percent of Ebeneezer's plans without ever trying them. But this time I held off, because when Ebeneezer is right, his plans (especially the ones for me) are solid. For instance, this book was his idea and so far that's worked out well, right?

So, that day I went down the rabbit hole that is mommy blogs and all I could think was, *Holy hell, what was he thinking? I am nothing like these women! This is a terrible plan! I knew it!*

These blogs were nothing like Ida's! I obviously did not understand what blogging was all about! I scrolled through endless pages of lies.

There was the mother who must secretly drink during nap time, because how else could you explain this kind of bullshit:

I love nothing more than baking with my two-year-old! It helps teach her dexterity, reading, and math. We're spending precious time

together and making #sweettreats and #memories.

There was the housewife who was dead inside and clearly wanted to kill herself:

It's Wednesday, ladies! It's Dust Day! My favorite day of week! Dust! Dust! Make that house sparkle and shine!

And there was the lunatic who cooked from scratch all day and probably had a full-size poster of June Cleaver serving Jesus dinner hanging in her pantry:

Cooking a healthy and nourishing meal for your family is the most empowering and Godly thing a woman can do. Nothing proves your love more, plus it gives you a sense of purpose and isn't that what we're all striving for?

"How's the blog coming?" Ebeneezer asked me later that day.

"Yeah, I'm not going to do that. I'm not a mommy blogger. Those women are deranged. They're clearly lying or on drugs or something. That shit's not real. And if it is, then I suck at being a wife and a mom and I want off the planet."

Ebeneezer shook his head. "Don't you get it? You're the anti-mommy blogger. You're the one who is going to tell the truth. You love being a wife and mom, but sometimes you want to move to a deserted island. You hate cooking and cleaning, and you'd rather read a smutty book than please your man. I'm willing to bet a lot of women feel the way you do. Besides, it doesn't matter.

You're writing for you. Just write what you feel. Get it down on paper and off your chest and you'll feel better. I promise."

I still wasn't convinced. "I don't know. I don't know anything about blogging. I haven't wanted to be a blogger since I was five years old. I've wanted to be an author! I want to write books."

"But books are hard," Ebeneezer said.

"How do you know?" I argued.

"Because you haven't written one," he said. "You've had years and you've done nothing."

I pouted. "I've been busy."

"Blogging is like baby steps, Jen. Maybe that's what you need to do. Maybe you need to ease into writing again through a blog?"

"Maybe," I said. "But they all have stupid cutesy names. What would I even call my blog? Jen's Jots? That's so lame."

"Oh, that part is easy," he said. "I've already thought of that. You should call your blog People I Want to Punch in the Throat because you say it all the time."

"Hmm...I kind of like it," I said, smiling, finally. "So, it's just a place where I can talk about my life or whatever? A place to vent?"

"Yes."

"But I'm not going to tell lies or humblebrag about my *ah-may-zing* life."

"Of course not. You're going to be yourself. I just can't listen to you complain anymore, so I need you to talk to the blog the way you talk to me. It's a win-win. You'll have alone time, and I won't worry about fixing you."

I considered that for a moment. "Okay. That I can do!"

I went online and found, much to my surprise, that

People I Want to Punch in the Throat dot com was still available, so I bought it and I started a blog.

I didn't talk about it. I didn't think about it. I didn't research how to start a blog. I just started.

I think this is where a lot of people get hung up. They want to talk and research how to blog or write a book, and that will just bog you down and overwhelm you.

That is literally my number one piece of writing advice: STOP TALKING AND START WRITING. If you take away nothing else from this book, let this be it.

I realized the easiest way to learn was through doing. You have to get started and figure it out as you go along. I didn't know anything about blogging when I started. I'd heard Ida and a few other people talk about Blogger and WordPress, but I really didn't know the difference between them.

I figured out Blogger was a free blogging platform and, for me, it was easier to work than WordPress, so I started there. I'm a complete tool when it comes to anything technological, so that should tell you how easy Blogger is to work. If I can do it, anyone can. Blogger isn't pretty, and it can't do a lot of fancy things, but for me it was perfect. I just wanted a free, easy site I could do on my own in my short free time.

So many people obsess over what their blog looks like, and I'm here to tell you it doesn't matter. You can have the ugliest blog in the world but if you have good content, people will read it. You don't need a pretty header or an adorable layout. Of course, if you have the money and/or the talent to make your site look good, go for it, but what I'm saying is don't let your lack of budget or design skills hold you back. Don't waste precious writing time making shit pretty. It doesn't matter how beautiful it looks; if there's no content, no one's coming.

My blog is ugly as shit and sparse. It has more words than images and it's dense. But people read the hell out of it.

When I created my blog, I had no idea there were rules or formats you were supposed to follow. I didn't have buttons or even an About Me section. No matter what, there are some important bits I should have had from the beginning:

1. **A Good Title.** You'll find all sorts of differing opinions on this one, but I stand by my advice to pick a good, unique, interesting title. There is a movement right now to name your blog after yourself. That YOU are your brand. And I get that and I believe that, too, but I still think your blog needs its own title. You are the creator of that blog, and you set the tone and the brand for the blog, but the blog is an extension of your brand. It should have a title that lets potential readers know what you're writing about. To me a blog is like a book. I would never call my book Jen Mann's Book, so why would I name my blog that? That doesn't tell a reader anything. They're like, "Who the hell is Jen Mann, and why do I care what she says?" But when a potential reader falls down the rabbit hole and onto my blog and sees PEOPLE I WANT TO PUNCH IN THE THROAT by Jen Mann, they know instantly if I'm their cup of tea or not. If they laugh, they stay. If they cringe and clutch their pearls, they move along.
2. **About Me.** This is where you give a brief bio of who you are and what your blog is all about. It's also where you can't be afraid to brag a bit

about what you've done and where you've been featured.

3. **Contact Me.** This is really important, because the goal is to get paid, right? None of us want to write for free forever, but if you don't have an email address, how are you going to find out about opportunities? Get yourself a dedicated email address that's just for the blog. Yes, you'll get some spam and some weirdo who will offer to pay you for pictures of your feet, but you'll also get dollars, so make sure you've got an email address that can be found easily and that you check OFTEN.

4. **Best Of.** I have more than six-hundred blog posts on my site now, and it can be a bit overwhelming for someone new. They might not have a clue who I am. Maybe they came in from an internet search or a link shared by a friend. I want them to stay and be a reader forever, but I can't guarantee that whatever post at the top of my blog is the best one. Let's face it, with six-hundred blog posts they can't all be amazeballs, and I don't want a random crappy one to be a new reader's first impression of me. So I have a list of my top ten most popular posts. Some of these posts might be five or six years old at this point, but who cares? They're new to this person. And I know they're my most-read posts. Stats don't lie. These are my winners. If the new people on my site don't like these, then I'm not for them.

5. **Subscribe Button.** Back in the day, everyone was sending their followers to the social media platforms like Facebook and Twitter, but now

those platforms limit your reach. They hold you hostage and demand you pay them to reach the people who chose to follow you. That's why I suggest you encourage them to subscribe. If your reader subscribes to your blog or newsletter, you can be sure it's delivered to their inbox and you're not beholden to the big platforms.
6. **Platform Follow Buttons.** Yeah, yeah. I know what I said above, but you need these guys too.

How You Can F*cking Do It:

- I said start already.
- Not sure where to start? Google that shit. And then start.

3

The Little Bastard That Changed My Life

"If you intend to write as truthfully as you can, your days as a member of polite society are numbered."

Stephen King

When I started People I Want to Punch in the Throat in April 2011 I would write whenever the mood struck me. I didn't have a plan. I wrote when I was irritated or when I had something to say. I would carve out a little time here and there to jot down my thoughts, but I didn't have a dedicated time to write or any sort of publishing schedule I adhered to. Hell, half the time I didn't even know my topic until I sat down! I didn't work on growing my social media (I didn't even know what social media was at that point) and I didn't care if my blog was read. In fact, I was writing my blog as if no one was reading it. I realize now that actually made me a bit freer in my writing and my style. I wasn't afraid what anyone would think, because I didn't think anyone knew my blog existed. I was truly writing only for myself and I was saying exactly what I wanted to say without any sort of filter or worry hanging over my head. I think that's a lot of the secret to my success. I was one hundred percent my authentic self. There was no bullshit and later on hundreds of thousands of readers would connect to that authenticity. Even now, eight years later, I'm still writing like that. I only care about the opinions of three people: my husband and my two kids. If they nix a topic or a story, I cut it, but no one else gets to have a say in what I write. I write for me and for my readers, no one else.

It was late one night during the first week of December when everything changed. We'd just gone to bed when Ebeneezer rolled over to look deep into my eyes and ask me, "What did you do today?"

I was going through that mental checklist every woman has in her head. I was moving everything that was on that day's list, but didn't get done, over to the next day's list. I was ticking imaginary boxes and I got to: MOVE THE ELF ON THE SHELF.

"Fuck," I groaned.

Now, let me stop right here and explain what the Elf on the Shelf is in case you have no idea what I'm talking about. He's this little magical doll that sits on a shelf in your house. He spies on your children and reports his findings to Santa. He's actually kind of handy, because when your kids are assholes you can tell them the elf is watching and they instantly behave. When the kids were little I thought about leaving the elf out all year round because he made them behave better. The elf watches the kid from his shelf during the day, and every night after they go to bed he flies back to the North Pole with his report for the

Big Guy. In order to make this believable to small children, an adult must move the doll from one shelf to another to prove he flew away. Personally, I think this part is stupid. Why can't he leave and land on the same shelf? Why must he always set up shop somewhere else in the house when we all know the mantle has the best views of all the action? Or it would be even better if he could sit on the shelf and transmit his message wirelessly to Santa without having to fly at all. Anyway, it doesn't matter. I didn't make the rules; I just had to make the magic happen and I kept forgetting.

"What's the matter?" Ebeneezer said.

"I forgot to move the elf," I said.

"Okay, so do it tomorrow," he said.

"I can't. The kids get up too early. He hasn't moved in, like, two days because I kept thinking I could do it in the morning before they came down. Today I accused Gomer of touching the elf and making him lose his magic."

"Jesus, Jen, he's only six, way to ruin him already."

"I know!" I shivered. It was cold and I was so cozy and sleepy in my bed. "Can you please move him?" I begged.

Ebeneezer shook his head. "No way. You know how I feel about all this Santa magic shit."

Ugh.

Ebeneezer is a truther. He *says* he hates lying to the kids. That they won't trust us, that he's not a liar, blah, blah. That part is true; I have never heard the Hubs lie to anyone (he's so truthful it can hurt sometimes), but I knew that wasn't his *real* issue with Christmas magic. He hates Santa. He hates that he's the one who buys and builds the dollhouse and the bicycle or whatever, but Santa gets all the credit. Santa gives the "good" presents and we give the kids socks and underwear. We look like chumps compared to Santa, and the Hubs hates looking like a chump.

"Come one. Just be a good dad," I whined. "Help me out."

"You know what? We can stop the madness and we have your laziness to thank."

"Pardon me?"

"This is perfect. We'll tell the kids the truth in the morning: there's no Santa, no Easter bunny, no tooth fairy, none of it! Our lives will be so much easier once we tell them the truth!"

I was horrified. "They're four and six! Talk about ruining them!"

He shrugged. "Look at me. I never believed in Santa, and I turned out just fine."

"Not true," I said, hauling myself out of bed. "You're a complete asshole."

I stumbled into the kitchen and found the elf on his dusty shelf. I moved him from the top shelf to the bottom shelf.

As I was leaving the kitchen I spotted my phone sitting on the counter. I hadn't been blogging long, but I'd been blogging long enough to know that if you do something and you don't put it on social media, it never happened. So, even though I was cold and tired and wanted nothing more than to crawl back into my bed, I snatched my phone and quickly typed an update.

It was a weeknight, probably after midnight or so and I wrote on Facebook: "Am I the only one forgetting to move my Elf on the Shelf?"

Within seconds my post was flooded with responses from other tired moms:

"I keep forgetting too!"

"Oh shoot! Thanks for the reminder, going now!"

"I just remembered!"

But there was a woman who had no children (and

some day when she does, I'm going to give her a puppy) posted: "I don't see what the big deal is, Moms, you just need a system!"

And she dropped a link to a blog with a list of a hundred-and-one things to do with your Elf on the Shelf. I opened the site and started reading. It was ideas like:

Trash your kitchen and say the elf made cookies. *(Tee hee hee.)*

My kitchen was already trashed! It would be more "magical" if the elf cleaned it!

Switch everyone's lunch and say the elf did it. *(Hilarious at school.)*

Hilarious until my kid has a hangry meltdown in the lunchroom because I've sent hummus instead of peanut butter.

Uh oh! The elf had a pillow fight. *(Feathers everywhere!*

1. Wait. We're trashing my house *again*? I'm beginning to see a theme here. I have enough work to do, and I don't need any more messes to clean up.
2. Do you have any idea what feather pillows cost??

I could feel the familiar sensation of anger bubbling up inside me. It was only the beginning of the holiday season, but already the pressure was mounting. It was all on me to do everything: decorate the house, buy the presents, wrap the presents, bake cookies, make crafts, go caroling—ALL OF IT. Moms are the ones who make the memories and make the season fucking magical, and I was failing miserably and this kind of bullshit wasn't helping. On top of the dread I could feel doubt creeping in. *Was* I ruining my kids because I couldn't remember to move the elf? *Fuuuuck.*

But then I felt another wave of rage take out any doubt. Who did this woman think she was with her hundred-and-one ideas? There are only twenty-five days of Christmas! It's already a magical time of year. I didn't need make myself unhinged to make it even more special!

No! I thought. *My kids are happy! And they are healthy! They are safe and they are loved! They have everything they need and more! I am a good mom, damn it, and I don't need to make a parachute out of a pair of underwear for a doll to prove it!!*

I let the fury boil over and basically possess me. And then I did what I did to make myself feel better: I wrote down what I was feeling.

I sat down at my laptop and I spit out a funny, honest (and irritated) response to this blogger and all the other perfect mommy bloggers like her. I railed against all the lies and the filtered glimpses of their lives they showed. They made their lives seem effortless and ideal. They never told you how hard it was to parent or be a wife. How hard it was to balance it all and look good doing it. No one showed you their dusty corners or their piles of laundry. No one told you how exhausted they were. I was tired of the lies. It was time for someone to tell the truth. I encouraged everyone reading to be done allowing with being made to feel less than because they were too tired or too overworked to go to all this trouble—and even when they did have the time or energy, maybe they just didn't want to do it, and that was okay too.

I don't know how long it took me, but I know it was

one of the fastest and easiest things I've ever written. I didn't self-edit or censor myself. I didn't worry about who might read it or who might be offended by my opinion. It wasn't about them; it was about *me* and how *I* felt. I just opened up my brain and my heart and I dumped it all on the page.

And then I felt better. *Ahhhhh.*

I shared it on my personal Facebook like I always did and I went to bed.

I know that during the next week something crazy happened, but it's been years since I've actually sat down and figured it all out. When I was writing this book I knew I wanted it to be as honest as possible, so I went back through my Facebook page. You know, the experts warn you that everything you put on these social media sites is forever, but it really is. I found every comment, every like, and every update from that insane week and I came up with an accurate timeline of what happened.

I wrote that post on December 9, 2011 and shared it with my three hundred or so friends on Facebook. I had seventy subscribers to my blog in those days, so they got a copy in their inbox. It was read about three hundred times, and then it sat there until a couple days later.

Ebeneezer went out to play poker that night and I was home alone with the kids. I'd put them to bed early and I was enjoying a beer and reading a book. My elf was sitting on his shelf staring at me.

The whole phenomena of posing elves in weird tableaus had just started, and I was trying to think of something funny to do with mine. So many of them were drinking hot cocoa or taking a marshmallow bubble bath. I wanted my elf to do something naughty.

I grabbed him off the shelf and draped his arm around the bottle of beer and snapped a picture. I uploaded it to my Facebook page and watched. Within a few minutes it had about twenty likes. That might not seem like a lot, but in those days my posts were getting between zero and five likes, so twenty was a lot.

I realized maybe I was onto something, so I added the picture to the blog post. I'd never put a picture on a blog post before. (Unless you were a DIY or food bloggers, it was still a rare thing to have a picture on a blog post. Since that night I've never hit publish without having one on there.) When I put his picture on the post, that's when it started to catch fire.

I attribute a lot of this to Pinterest. Pinterest came into existence the year before, but that winter, because it was full of seasonal decorations, recipes, crafts, and more, the platform was really catching fire with "normal" people like me. I didn't have a Pinterest account, but I'd at least heard of it. If you want a blog post to end up on Pinterest, it needs an image for a user to "pin" to their boards. Anyone can pin your blog post and then their followers see the picture, and when they click, it sends them to your blog post. My friends had done a decent job sharing the link with their friends on Facebook, but I think Pinterest was the game-changer.

The next day I wrote a status update on Facebook marveling over the fact that I had twelve hundred reads on my elf post—more than every post on the entire blog combined at that point.

Two days later I was sitting in a PTA board meeting at school when I got a text message from the Hubs. (Yeah, I joined the PTA. I told you I needed to get out of my house.)

HUBS: SOMETHING WEIRD W/YOUR BLOG.
ME: I'M VERY BUSY. NOT NOW. ME TIME!

HUBS: OK, BUT YOU HAVE LOTS OF COMMENTS.

It wasn't unusual for him to know about comments coming in because like I said, we shared a small office and we share several email accounts. So he could hear my notifications dinging on my laptop, and he took a look at our email accounts to see which one was blowing up. I know he was hoping it was one of our real estate ones with a bunch of potential million-dollar buyers, but instead he found it was the one linked to my blog. Every time I get a comment on the blog, Blogger sends me an email. When I get five comments, it's no big deal, but I was getting hundreds, so my notifications were going wild.

ME: PROBABLY SPAMMERS.
HUBS: I DON'T THINK SO.
ME: BUSY!!!
HUBS: OK. I'LL FIGURE IT OUT.

Up until that point Ebeneezer hadn't taken much interest in my blog except to ask *if* I was writing, not so much *what* I was writing. He never read what I wrote, he didn't help me set it up, he didn't share it, but now that it was annoying him, he was interested.

He downloaded Google Analytics so he could see what was happening. I didn't know what Google Analytics was back then. I know now it's an accurate way to track your website's statistics. He could use Google Analytics to see how many people were on my site in real-time, where they were located, and which links were bringing them in.

HUBS: YOU HAVE 5K PEOPLE READING ELF POST.

ME: HOW DO YOU KNOW?
HUBS: GOOGLE ANALYTICS.
ME:???
HUBS: 7K!
ME: YOU BROKE MY BLOG!
HUBS: HOLY SHIT 10K.

I continued to run the meeting as my phone chimed with text message updates from the Hubs, but once we got to about twenty thousand readers I was like, "Meeting adjourned, bitches! I'm going viral!"

Little did I know that was just the beginning

How You Can F*cking Do It:

- Write about your experiences.
- Be authentic, honest, vulnerable, and brave.
- Share on social media.
- Track your results.

4

F*Ck Fear

> **"Write what disturbs you, what you fear, what you have not been willing to speak about. Be willing to be split open."**
>
> Nattalie Goldberg

I rushed home and watched the analytics all afternoon and into the night.

I knew something was up the next day when friends were sending me messages saying things like, "My friend in Maine who has no idea who you are just sent me your blog to read! I was like, 'Duh, I went to college with her!'" At one point a friend who worked for Yahoo messaged me to say, "You are going viral. I'm seeing your blog everywhere!"

Now, remember this was before the BuzzFeeds of the world existed. Nowadays you go viral and there are hundreds of online outlets to pick you up and amplify the message. Ida went viral a few years ago, and it was insane how many different outlets around the world picked up the story and shared it. Times have really changed! Back when I was going viral, Yahoo was really all there was, and for them to think I was viral made me realize something big was happening.

When the page views reached one hundred sixteen thousand, I started a Facebook page for People I Want to Punch in the Throat and encouraged people to follow me there.

I did this because I had so many people reaching out to me and it freaked me out, but I didn't want to ignore them either. I had hundreds of friend requests on my personal Facebook account, and I was terrified to accept any of them. I even had people tracking down my real estate website and sending me emails there. I received emails through friends of friends.

Ninety-nine percent of the comments and messages I received were positive, but there are some crazy motherfuckers out there, and that was my first experience with that nonsense. When I created that Facebook page for the blog, I did it more as a buffer between me and the public. The Hubs quickly figured out how to put a big follow button on the blog and right away we got thousands of followers.

After I got the Facebook page up and running, Ida texted me.

IDA: DUDE, YOU'RE ALL OVER TWITTER!
ME: WTF IS THE TWITTER?

I had no idea what Twitter was, but I figured it out pretty fast. I created a Twitter account and managed to grab a few followers over there too. The thing about Twitter, though, is it's never been my cup of tea. I'm way too wordy for Twitter, and my readers don't like it either. At the end of the day, for better or for worse, we're Facebook people. I created a Pinterest account too so I could pin my post and get some page views on my own. In those days those three were really the only platforms anyone cared about, so I quit there. I still wasn't thinking of these platforms as promotional tools, because at that point I didn't know I'd be needing any promotional tools. I really thought I'd be a one-hit wonder and someday we'd all laugh about that one time Jen almost broke the internet.

Ebeneezer and I were glued to the computer watching the numbers rise on Google Analytics. It was later that day that Ebeneezer wrote on my Facebook timeline:

Congratulations, one million reads on the Elf on the Shelf post!

When I went viral, I was prepared to let it run and enjoy my taste of fame for a day or two and then go back into obscurity but thank goodness the Hubs had another plan. "Okay, you've crossed one million reads on the Elf on the Shelf post," he said that fateful December night. "What are you going to do tomorrow?"

I stopped rocking, crying, and breathing into a paper bag long enough to say, "Tomorrow? Are you crazy! I'll never top this!"

The Hubs shrugged. "Yeah, probably not." (I told you, the Hubs is a truther. He's never the guy you want to ask if your ass looks big in a new pair of jeans.)

"What if this is it?" I wailed.

"I don't think it is. I think you can do something with this. I think you can turn this into something bigger."

"Really?"

He nodded. "Yes. It's not going to be a million reads every day, but this is a gift. This is your chance. Are you really going to waste it, or are you going to seize it and see what you can do?"

"What if I fail?" I whispered.

He shrugged and said, "So what if you do? We'll still be here. You'll still have your real estate business. It won't ruin anything if you fail."

I struggled to spit out the words, "But I'll be a ... failure."

He shrugged again. "You'll be a failure who actually took a shot!" he said. "At this point you're just a failure who never even tried. Is that what you want, Jen?"

I'd never thought of failure that way before. He was right; I was ready to give up before I even tried to succeed. I was prepared to give up. AGAIN. I was letting fear control me. I was letting fear take over.

"I'll never get a million reads again," I said, still afraid.

"Stop being afraid!" the Hubs ordered. "Come on, how many people are following you now?"

I checked my newly created Facebook account. "Around seventeen thousand," I said.

"Seventeen thousand people, Jen. Do you have any idea how many people that is? Think about it. That's more than some stadiums can hold! That's crazy. And you can grow it—we can grow it."

"We?" I asked. "You've never been interested in helping me grow my blog before."

He nodded. "I know. But I am now. We can find more people to follow you and turn this into a career for you."

"A career? What kind of career?" I asked, still not catching on.

"Do you remember what you told me on our first date?" the Hubs asked.

"No."

"You told me you wanted to be a writer. This is your chance! You have seventeen thousand people who want to hear from you! I can see the stats. They're reading your archives. They're devouring everything you have on the blog. They want more from you! But you have to start now. You can't wait, because they won't wait."

I felt the pangs of fear and doubt creep in. "But what would I even write?" I whimpered.

"Entertain them," he said, encouraging me. "Make them laugh. Tell them more funny stories. You can do this, Jen."

I was paralyzed with fear. I couldn't imagine anything other than crashing and burning. I've never been a person who craved the spotlight or wanted fame. I wanted to write, but I didn't want to be famous. I wanted to be known for my work, but I didn't want to actually talk to people or hear critiques of my work. But I realized I couldn't have it both ways. If I wanted to be a successful writer, I was going to have to push down that fear and those insecurities and embrace the unknown. I was going to have to try new things and know that not everything would work. They can't all be winners. I was going to have to take chances and be vulnerable and brave. And maybe even fail.

I can't do it, I thought. My college professor who told me I'd never amount to anything popped into my head. I remembered his cruel words to me, "You should give up on writing and just become someone's wife."

I'd like to tell you I reached down deep inside and found my bravery and I said, "Fuck fear" and I overcame my insecurities and got to work. Instead, I realized that night I'm motivated by a healthy dose of fire and revenge. So I reached deep down inside myself and harnessed that rage and said, "Fuck that guy." And I started writing.

How You Can F*cking Do It:

- Capitalize on the luck.
- Find your motivation and what drives you.
- Get to work.

5

Make Some Rules

"Daring to set boundaries is about having the courage to love ourselves even when we risk disappointing others."

Brené Brown

When the Elf on the Shelf post went viral I was too busy rocking in a corner and breathing into a paper bag to celebrate. I don't know, maybe you've had one million reads on one post on your blog, but I hadn't been through that and it's a very surreal experience. I know we tell our kids that everything they put on the internet can be found by other people, blah, blah, blah, but we don't really believe it. There's a shit-ton of content on the internet, and what are the chances the sun and moon and stars are going to line up just perfectly so that one million people stumble onto your little corner of the online world?

And as a writer, of course I wanted people to read my work, but I wanted them to read my polished, intelligent, thought-provoking, life-changing work. I wanted to be known for my amazing prose and complex storytelling, not a rant about a stupid elf! My blog was where I farted around and cracked jokes while I contemplated writing the Great American Novel. I didn't consider the blog to be my "real" writing, and I was a bit embarrassed that's what took off.

Spoiler alert: I've since stopped being so fucking precious about my writing and realized I was a dumbass for even stressing about this. Over the years I received so many notes from people thanking me for saying exactly what they were thinking. They thank me for validating their feelings and for making them feel like they aren't alone. They thank me for making them laugh during stressful times in their lives. Many are feeling the pressures of parenting or holidays or just the world, but I've also heard from people going through divorces, mothers who've lost children, families going through major health crises. I realized early on, those are the people I'm talking for. Yes, my blog is silly and stupid at times, but I'm bringing joy to people's lives. I don't want to be known for literary masterpieces (I mean, if that happens, great, but it's not my goal anymore). I want to be known as the writer who will bring relief and happiness to your life. There is nothing I love more than hearing that for just a few minutes I made someone's shitty day brighter. I want to make people laugh. I want to make them think. I want to make them rage or cry. We're all so numb, and I want to make people feel something.

The truth is, I'm never going to be Donna Tartt, so I might as well embrace who I am: Erma Bombeck with F-bombs.

I was also extremely preoccupied with the "haters." As I said before, the vast majority of the comments were positive, but there were a few that really got under my (very thin) skin. I'd never been publicly criticized before. And they weren't even criticizing my grammar (which would have been fair). Instead, they were criticizing my thoughts and views on the world, or they were sticks in the mud who couldn't take (or understand) a joke, but the worst were the ones who threatened my children.

When the threats to my kids came through, that was when I was done. I was ready to close up shop and finally move to that cabin off the grid.

A few women told me I was an unfit and lazy mother and they'd come to Kansas, figure out which school my children attended, steal them, and raise them surrounded by elves and magic every day. My kids were only four and six and would have gone off willingly with anyone with a puppy or an ice cream sandwich. Even more women told me I didn't deserve children and maybe I'd like to know the pain of losing a child, because that could be arranged. And let's not forget the men who threatened to rape me. The bulk of the haters were worried about my husband being married to such a fucking harpy and offered to pray for him.

Holy shit! All I did was complain about moving my Elf on the Shelf! Calm the fuck down, everybody!

You can say all you want about me. You can call me names or make threats against me, but they came for my children, you guys! My children! **OH HELL NO!** I will end you. As much as I wanted to run away and hide, I also wanted to fight. I had a small, intensely loyal army at my disposal. One word from me and I could ruin the lives of these haters. I wanted to unleash the power of my thousands of new followers on these trolls with orders to bring me back photographs, social security numbers, addresses, phone numbers, and the names of their next of kin. I wanted to scare them so bad their mothers would call me and apologize for their upbringing and beg me for mercy. I wanted to nuke their homes and pave the rubble so I'd have an extra place to park my car.

But I didn't do that, because I'm not a lunatic!

Here's the thing: I don't care what people have written about you, you do not unleash hell on them. You don't go around doxxing people. If you're feeling threatened, call the police, call the FBI, but don't fire up an online horde into a frenzy. I've seen this happen way too many times, and it almost never goes well for the organizer. There are no rules in a mob, and people will get hurt and it will be your fault.

The thing to remember about these trolls or haters or whatever you want to call them, most of the time they are sad, damaged people who have nothing better to do than try and make you feel bad about yourself. I imagine them in their mother's dank basements, wearing nothing but grungy underwear and tapping away insults at me with Cheetos-covered fingers on an old, rickety computer.

Earlier this year, I saw where Patton Oswalt was attacked on Twitter. This is not unusual for him. Patton Oswalt has strong opinions that he shares freely and publicly. But when this man attacked, instead of fighting back, Patton decided to find out more about him. One quick search revealed this man was suffering. He'd had some health issues and he wasn't doing well. In addition to poor health, he was drowning in medical bills and he had set up a GoFundMe. Instead of asking his army of followers to ruin this man, Patton Oswalt asked his people to help him support this man. Together they exceeded the five-thousand-dollar goal and changed this man's heart. THAT is the kind of power the internet has, and THAT is how it should be used.

So, instead of exacting my revenge, I quickly took everyone's real names off my blog and any photographs of my family on social media were made private. I gave my kids the horrible fake names Gomer and Adolpha and they've never forgiven me. The kids' names were chosen randomly from a book of twenty thousand baby names I've had on my desk most of my life. The Hubs became Ebeneezer, because he's a Scrooge, so that one made sense. I kept Jen, because I couldn't imagine being someone else.

I went deep underground. I kept writing, but I refused to show my face or pictures of my family. I refused to disclose where we lived. I always used fake names. I threatened anyone who knew me in real life to carry our secrets to their graves. These were the boundaries the Hubs and I set that night. We agreed that no matter what, we'd try to keep my two lives as separate as possible. I was the one who wanted to write. I was the one who wanted to put my opinions out there. My kids didn't sign up for that, and I wanted to protect them as best I could, while still doing what I needed to do for myself.

I've been very clear with my readers since that first night about my boundaries. Over time, I've loosened the reins a bit. When I self-published *Spending the Holidays with People I Want to Punch in the Throat* in 2012, I listed Jen of People I Want to Punch in the Throat as the author. It wasn't until Penguin Random House published *People I Want to Punch in the Throat: Competitive Crafters, Drop-Off Despots, and Other Suburban Scourges* two years later that I put my face and full name on a book for the first time. A few years after that I began speaking publicly or on camera.

I've still managed to keep my kids under wraps. Now that they're older they have their own social media accounts and I'm letting them pick and choose what they'll share with the world. Gomer's quite shy and doesn't want much attention, but Adolpha would have a one-woman variety show if I'd let her. Neither is impressed with me and what I've accomplished, so I guess I'm doing something right!

A lot of writers ask me how I'm able to maintain these boundaries and I will say it can be exhausting and you do miss out on opportunities. I've said no when national news crews wanted to come to my house and film my family. There have been times international press coverage has been denied because I wouldn't reveal my last name. And I've been pitched more than one reality show about my family. A reality show is literally the last thing I want. Yes, I want a television show based on People I Want to Punch in the Throat, but not a reality show.

We missed out on a lot, but we were convinced partial anonymity was more important than any benefit we might get from lowering our standards. Maintaining your boundaries is a lot like parenting—you must put up a united front and be willing to die on that hill. My readers caught on quickly too, especially once I told them I was worried about my kids' safety and privacy. Most of them are parents, too, so they understood completely.

In fact, they now help me enforce my rules. A few years ago I was traveling with my family and I was giving a speech at a library. Normally I'd be on my own, but since it was spring break, I was traveling with the family. The Hubs and the kids accompanied me to the library. They were going to hang out and read some books while I gave my speech and then we'd go out after for ice cream or something if they were good.

We arrived early and the Hubs and the kids helped me set up my books and PowerPoint. The librarian who had invited me to speak met them all, but she didn't know my rules. When she introduced me to the attendees later that evening, she read my bio, and it mentions my husband and kids. She stopped and said something like, "Actually, I met Jen's family tonight. Her kids are here in the building somewhere."

A woman in the audience perked up and got a wild look in her eye. I wasn't afraid of her, though, because I recognized that look. Not everyone wants to steal or hurt my children. There are just some people out there who have a genuine curiosity about my kids and want to know more about them. She looked poised to get up and go find them when the woman behind her put a gentle but firm hand on her shoulder and said, "No. Gomer and Adolpha are private. We leave them alone."

The wild-eyed woman relaxed immediately and said, "You're right. I'm sorry. Thanks for reminding me."

If you let your boundaries be known and you enforce them on a regular basis, it will get easier. I think if you're honest and communicate with your audience, they will understand. We've all got a right to privacy and when you explain it that way, most people respect your lines in the sand.

Some people just won't take no for an answer, though. Every now and again someone will say to me, "It's okay, I'm your biggest fan. I won't tell anyone. What are Gomer and Adolpha's real names?"

There's no point arguing with them because they won't be deterred. I don't want to be rude, though, because they're my "biggest fan," so I've found over the years that humor works well in this situation. I'll laugh and say, "Oh, I can't tell you—because they're actually *worse*."

How You Can F*cking Do It:

- Figure out your boundaries.
- Enforce them like a mofo.

6

Cool Story, Jen, But How Do I Go Viral?

"People will forget what you said, people will forget what you did, but people will never forget how you made them feel."

Maya Angelou

I tell you what, if I knew the secret to going viral, I'd do it every single week! Actually, lots of people think it's something that just happens organically, but that's not exactly true. It can be designed and orchestrated. It's just not that easy to pull off. I'll give you a recipe you can follow, but you probably still need that spark of luck to set it into motion.

First, let's decide what "viral" means. Everyone has a different definition of what viral means. The number I've seen thrown around a lot is ten times your normal traffic. Personally, I think ten times is a bit low. With some work, most people can achieve ten times their traffic fairly easy.

To call it a "viral post," I'd say it needs to be at least fifty to a hundred times your normal traffic.

And people can be picky about *where* you go viral. These days it's easier to go viral on certain platforms versus others, so that gets taken into account too. For instance, I see lots of embedded, long-form posts or videos on Facebook, Instagram, and YouTube going viral these days and garnering hundreds of thousands, if not millions, of page views. I've also seen original essays on *Medium*, *The New York Times*, or *The Washington Post* break out. What I don't see a lot of anymore are blog posts from freestanding sites going viral unless they've been reposted on larger aggregate sites with huge built-in audiences. That's because it's getting harder than ever to get your audience to leave the big platforms, because Facebook and Instagram don't like to show links that encourage their users to leave their site.

When I wrote the Elf on the Shelf post I had seventy subscribers to my blog and no social media following except my three hundred or so personal friends and family on Facebook. Because that post was read by over one million people in twenty-four hours, there's no question it was viral.

Since then I've had other posts go viral too. None were as big as the Elf, but many were read and shared hundreds of thousands of times. A few months after I went viral, Ebeneezer and I decided to break it down and figure out what happened exactly and if we could recreate it in the future. Here's what we found:

Your post needs to be topical. Notice I didn't say "original." People always think they need an original topic, but they don't. I'll hear people complain that "everything's been said" on a particular topic, and that's not true. You haven't had your say yet. Your story, your experience, and your voice are different. You just need an original spin on an already popular topic.

Let's look at my Elf on the Shelf post. I wrote that post during the first week of December, so the Elf on the Shelf was already a popular topic. People were talking about it and thinking about it because it was in "season." That was also the first year the Elf on the Shelf doll was widely available online and in big box stores so more people had one. They were making their elves do over-the-top ridiculous antics and sharing the posts on social media. My spin wasn't yet another adorable tableau of my elf making snow angels in a pile of powdered sugar. My spin was I am a good enough mother and I don't need to make a parachute out of a pair of underwear for a doll to prove it!

Your post needs to be relatable. Readers want to see themselves in what you write. They want to identify on a personal level. Christmas is a lot of pressure for moms. Women felt that pressure, but they were keeping it under wraps and no one really wanted to talk about it. By being honest about my feelings, I connected to the women suffering in silence. I made them feel like they weren't alone. It also didn't hurt that I was one of the first bloggers to call bullshit on what the fake perfection mommy bloggers were throwing out there. I was one of the first to pull back the veil and show the truth.

You post needs to be easy to read and conversational. Imagine you're having a conversation with a friend. That's the way you should be writing. Forget your fifty-cent words; no one's impressed by them and no one wants a dictionary to read what you've written. Keep the tone friendly and let your personality shine through. I'm snarky, sweary, and funny, but *you* don't have to be that way. You do you. If you're sweet and bubbly, then let that come across in your writing. Find your own voice and stick with it.

Your post needs to be easy to share. This goes back to the buttons you need on your blog. Make them big and bold so they can't be missed and so it's easy to share your hilarious/heartwarming/informative post and make it go viral.

This recipe might sound disheartening, but fear not, it's not impossible to go viral!

My sister-in-law, Ida, did it recently. She was a bridesmaid twenty-some years ago and the bride shared a picture of the bridal party with an offhand apology about the ugly dresses she made her friends wear. Since Ida doesn't part with anything (nor does her ass get any bigger, apparently) she still had her dress. She dug it out and put it on. She had her kids snap a few quick pictures of her in the dress doing chores around the house: folding laundry, watering the garden, that sort of thing. She shared the photos and said something like, "What are you talking about? I wear mine all the time!"

As soon as I saw those photos, I knew Ida could go viral. Whether she meant to or not, she had the right recipe. The pictures were relatable because how many of us have ugly, twenty-year-old bridesmaid dresses hanging in our closets? It was also aspirational, because how many of us can still fit into those twenty-year-old dresses? It was funny. The juxtaposition of a middle-age woman in a retro formal gown with tennis shoes doing the dishes is hilarious. And it was a photo versus a story. Photos are easily shared and understood across all languages.

Ida is normally a private person, so her settings are always set to Friends Only. You can't go viral unless your post is public. People have to be able to share it.

I sent Ida a message: MAKE THOSE PICS PUBLIC AND LET'S BLOW UP THE INTERNET.

Neither of us knew at the time, but the bride's profile was public, so they were already starting to trend. But once she made the pictures public, they were off like wildfire before I could even share them. They were picked up by legitimate news organizations as well as bizarro internet sites no one's ever heard of. During the next few days the pictures were featured everywhere, and she was interviewed by a few of the publications as well as local and national television news shows.

At one point she asked me how to handle it all. "It depends on what you want," I said. As I said before, Ida had been a blogger, but she'd quit years ago and I didn't know why. "Do you want to reboot your blog?"

"I don't think so," she said. "It was fun when my kids were little, but they're older now. I don't want to start blogging again just to make this into something bigger."

"Do you want a book deal?" I knew Ida had dozens of old bridesmaid dresses in her closet and I could see pitching a book of nothing but photos of her grocery shopping or mowing the yard in twenty-year-old formal gowns.

"No, not really," she said.

"So what do you want?" I asked.

"I'd kind of like to get on *Ellen*" she said wistfully.

"Yeah ... that's going to take some work," I said. "Blogging, tweeting, pimping yourself hard to catch her eye. Are you up for that?"

Ida considered it but in the end she decided she didn't want this to become her job. She didn't care about notoriety or fame. She wanted to make people laugh a bit and then go back to her normal, private life. And that's okay too, because not everyone wants to be famous. Ida didn't orchestrate this event; it happened to her, and in the end, she didn't want anything other than to have a little fun. And she did.

Sometimes you might go viral for the wrong reasons or you might go viral for something you didn't expect. When you're in the throes of a viral hit, it might seem like it will never end and the spotlight will be on you forever, but that's not true. Yes, it's all out there, and if I Googled Ida I'd find the pictures and stories all over again, but to the normal internet user, she's now forgotten. People have moved on and her moment has passed. She didn't want anything other than that moment, so she did the right thing, but if you want to turn that chance into something bigger, you have to be ready to get to work.

How You Can F*cking Do It:

- Find your voice.
- Follow the formula.
- Watch for an opportunity and seize it.

7

Get To Work

"You own everything that happened to you. Tell your stories. If people wanted you to write warmly about them, they should've behaved better."

Anne Lamott

After I went viral, I had a choice. I could either sit back and wait to see what happened, or I could be proactive and take charge of my future. I wanted to get to work. I made a commitment to write five times a week on the blog, but with a full-time job and two small children, I wasn't sure when I'd find the time write.

I figured out that I was most productive late at night when everyone was asleep and the house was quiet. "How about you stay up late to write and I'll get up with the kids in the morning so you can sleep in a bit?" Ebeneezer suggested.

(If I haven't mentioned it yet, now would be a good time to say that my husband is a goddamn saint. Seriously. If you don't have a partner who will support you in this whole writing thing, you're going to have a much harder time. Writing can be a time—and money—suck without a lot of payoff, especially right away, so a supportive spouse is critical in your success. Plus, writing is tough on the soul. Rejection, self-doubt, and negativity are huge parts of this business and when I am at my lowest, it is my husband who bolsters me and re-energizes me and reminds me of the big picture and what I'm trying to accomplish and puts me back on track.)

I wanted to get a lot done in a day, and I needed a plan that would work for me. I was still selling real estate and trying to take care of my family, so I got in the habit of time blocking. Time blocking allowed me to could carve out some writing time as well. I'd been taught time blocking when I first started selling real estate. Real estate is a solitary business where you have to be self-motivated. You don't really have anyone telling you what to do and if you don't work, you don't get paid, so you have to manage your time efficiently and effectively. Real estate is project-based and deadline-based rather than a typical hourly job. You have a goal you're working toward, and it's best to plan backward. You have to figure out what needs to get done and when it needs to get done by and how much you need to work every day in order to meet your deadline. You have to work on current projects as well as always be looking toward the future for new projects. You have to manage updates and deadlines and there are consequences if you miss those deadlines. You have to generate leads and network with others in your industry and keep up to date on best business practices. Real estate is one hundred percent commission-based, so no salary. If you're not producing, you're not eating.

Writing can be a lot like this too and time blocking will help. In those early writing days I worked on real estate for the bulk of my day, I'd stop for dinner with the family, hang out with them in the evening, put the kids to bed, and then spend about an hour with my husband either watching television or talking or finishing work that didn't get done earlier in the day. He'd go to bed around ten or eleven and I'd stay up and write, answer emails, update my social media accounts, and more.

I would typically work on one blog post at time. A blog post would take me about three hours to write. I have no idea if this is standard. I write about twelve hundred words per blog post, which is not standard. That is long. Most experts will tell you that's too long. Three hundred to five hundred words is a good length for a blog post. I've always been wordy, so I need three hundred words just to set up the story! I've always managed to keep people reading even when I write longer blog posts. I think that as long as you're telling a good story, people will read whatever you've written. In those days I was selling real estate seven days a week and blogging five days a week, so I really didn't have the time to write several blog posts in advance and then dole them out, but I know a lot of bloggers who do that. They might take an entire Saturday or Sunday and write a week's worth of posts at once. This style is very efficient and effective for some people, but it just doesn't work for me. I am a really organic writer. Yes, writing is a j-o-b for me, but I also have to be inspired to write something. I can't just sit down and come up with fifteen topics and write about them. I need something to happen to me or I need to read something that moves me and then I must sit down right then and write about it before the moment is gone. That's why I always carry a notebook or my laptop with me. I'm always jotting down something I want to remember. If you can crank out a bunch of content in advance, I encourage you to do so, because it will make your life so much easier.

Instead I would stay up until about two o'clock in the morning writing about whatever was on my mind. This is also what makes my blog unique. Back when I started blogging, they all had "themes." They were about crafts or recipes or home making or parenting. They adhered to rigid rules. "My blog is about hot dogs, so I can only post about hot dogs! Hot dog reviews are fine. Hot dog recipes are fine. But holiday crafts are bad—unless I'm making a wreath out of hot dogs!" Those rigid rules can be tough for some, and that's why you're seeing a trend right now where everyone is converting their blogs to "lifestyle" blogs. Lifestyle blogs are good because the writer can cover a lot of topics like personal essays, fashion, design, crafts, recipes, and it all makes sense, because it's what's important to the blogger.

My blog, People I Want to Punch in the Throat, isn't considered a lifestyle blog, but it is all about me (my favorite subject), and I have no rules other than tell a good story and make it funny. But I break those rules a lot too. My blog is my safe space. It's where I dump my brain and my heart. It's where I entertain people with stories about myself and my family. It's where I rail and rage against the injustices I see in the world. It's where I educate, inform, and entertain my readers. One day I will recommend my favorite books and cozy leggings, the next day I will tell a hilarious story about my kids, and the next day I will eviscerate a politician or celebrity or my neighbor. Nothing is off limits on my blog. This is not a path I would recommend for everyone, though. It's polarizing and sometimes it causes a lot of chaos on the blog. I gain and lose followers every day. People flounce out the door and call me names, others send me hateful or violent messages. But I don't give a fuck. The way I see it is I'm not everybody's cup of tea and that's okay. I don't need to change so some stranger in Nebraska will like me better. I don't need to tone down my language so some dude in Florida will think I'm ladylike. Fuck that noise.

I say and do what I want. I didn't ask for anyone else's opinion, except the Hubs and my kids—they're the only ones with veto power. I didn't ask for anyone's permission. I don't have an employer who can fire me for speaking my mind. I don't have friends and family who will disown me if they disagree with me.

When I'm writing, I'm only writing for me and the people who need to hear me at that exact moment. I'm only speaking to them. To the ones who need to laugh, or be seen, or need to cry, or whatever it is they need, I'm there for them that day.

Over the years I've developed an incredibly thick skin and nothing really hurts me anymore. I don't watch my numbers and fret over how many people I'm losing (or gaining). I don't cry when I read the comments. The only ones that hurt a little are the ones who I recognize as longtime readers. After a while those readers feel like friends to me and so it's a tad painful when they draw the line in the sand and they leave. But you know what, if they're going to defend a rapist or a leave me over my opinion about pumpkin spice, then they were never my friend to begin with, and I was completely wrong to consider them one.

I'm not normal, though. If you want as many eyeballs as possible with as few fights as possible, then I'd stick to fashion or crafts or recipes. Although, be warned, people will always find something to bitch about: "Are you really endorsing a six-hundred-dollar umbrella? AYFKM? Must be nice to be so out of touch!" or "Where's the trigger warning for the glue gun? I had a horrible experience with a glue gun a few years ago and I can't even look at a glue stick without breaking out into hives! I won't be back!" or "Great recipe! If you want to kill your family from heart disease! Canned vegetables? Condensed soup? This isn't food, this is BIG AGRA DEATH!"

Basically, the internet is the Wild West and you have to buck up if you're going to do this. I have several ways I get through the negativity.

Read the comments. Hear me out. I know a lot of people will tell you to NEVER read the comments, but I disagree. If you don't read the comments, you're living in your own echo chamber of fanboys and fangirls. You have to read the comments and take the feedback you're receiving. You should read to see if you missed something. Many times I'm writing so fast and furious that *I* think I'm making my position clear, but when others read it, they're not getting it. That's the nice thing about blogging: you can edit. I go back and edit my posts to clarify points so that I'm better understood. I'm not saying you need to give oxygen to the trolls. No one needs to read the "go kill yourself" comments, but you should definitely read the comments that give you a different perspective and at least "hear" what they have to say. Yes, my opinion is strong, but my opinion is not set in stone. I am teachable. I can change. My outlook on a lot of things has changed a lot since I started blogging, and I thank the internet for that. I meet people I would normally never meet and I hear their stories and they move me. Read the positive comments. THOSE are your people. Read the comments from the people who get you and/or needed to hear what you were saying. I always say that I speak for those who can't speak for themselves. For one reason or another, they can't raise their voice, so I raise mine. Those are the people who leave me comments or send me emails thanking me.

Put on your blinders and stay in your lane. There's a lot going on out there, and it's easy to be distracted. It's easy to compare yourself to others and worry that maybe you're not doing as well as they are. You might see something that works for one writer and you think, "I should do that too!" but deep down you know it's not your thing. And what works for one writer might not work for you. You know what you do best, stick to it, and find the people who like you for you.

Embrace the negativity. I've built a cottage industry on The Art of the Rant. Some days my life is too fucking great for me to write. I need to be pissed off to write. I need that visceral emotion. Half the time I'm shaking with anger and/or crying when I'm writing. As the Emperor would say, "Let the hate flow through you."

Remember why you're doing this. Keep your eye on the prize. Big picture. All that shit. Some people need a vision board or a quote to keep them centered. Figure out what you need and make that your North Star and always be working toward that goal, every single day, no excuses.

Take a break. This isn't a sprint, it's a marathon, and you've allowed to take a rest.

Laugh. I'm a big believer that laughter cures just about everything. When I'm feeling particularly stressed, I go out and find things to make me laugh and then I feel better.

Now that I've quit my job and I'm writing full-time; my schedule is a lot more open. But I still use time blocking. I get asked a lot about my typical day, so here you go:

7:30 a.m.: Check all my emails on my phone in my bed while the Hubs gets kids out the door. I have four email accounts and they can be accessed from all my devices. I don't reply unless it only requires a yes or no, because I don't like to type a lot on my phone.

8:00 a.m.: Reply to urgent emails and my Virtual Assistant. Add items to my calendar and my to-do list. (My calendar is a shared Google calendar with the Hubs and the kids. We can all see and add to it. This helps me stay organized and able to plan events and meetings without having to waste a lot of time conferring with everyone else. I am one of those relics with a paper to-do list. It's a spiral notebook that I continually update. I've tried virtual lists, but I'm a pen-and-paper kind of gal.) I continually check email throughout the day and into the night. If I need to book flights, hotels, cars, events, etc., now is the time to do it. I like to get all my planning and office work out of the way first thing in the morning.

9:00 a.m. – noonish: It's social media time. The Hubs calls this my "play time," but it's actually really important. I check in on all my platforms and answer private messages, reply to comments, like, share, interact, network, etc. I use secret boards on Pinterest to save things I want to share across my different pages. I pick and choose from these boards depending upon my mood. I also will find topical articles or memes to share. I like to ask open-ended questions or tell stories to get people talking. This is also when I will write a newsletter or an email for my Super Friends. I try to schedule any interviews or podcasts during this time so it doesn't interfere with my writing time later in the day.

Noonish – Whenever: It's go time. Some people like to get up at the ass crack of dawn to write, but that doesn't spark joy (thank you, Marie Kondo) for me. I can't concentrate on writing when my inbox is taunting me. I prefer to get all my busywork out of the way, and then get down to the serious business of writing. I am almost always working on a project and depending upon the stage it's in, I have plenty of work to do. Sometimes it might be a word count I'm trying to hit. When I come up with a new book I work backward from my deadline and figure out how many words I need to write every day to get it done on time. Sometimes it's three thousand words, sometimes it's six thousand words. Or it could be editing or formatting that needs to be done that day. Whatever the task, I don't quit until I'm done. I aim for dinner time, but that doesn't always work.

4:00 p.m.-ish – 9:00 p.m.: Take a break and fix dinner, hang out with family, etc. Check social media, emails, etc., on the phone.

11 p.m.: Back to work. But this is only sometimes. I'm a fool when it comes to my deadlines. I am only motivated by fear of failure, so I've got to set hard-and-tight (that's what she said) deadlines for myself. I actually really enjoy working late into the night. My house is quiet, my inbox and social media are quiet, my brain is quiet. I can get a fuck-ton of work done between 11 p.m. and 2 a.m.

How You Can F*cking Do It:

- Write consistently.
- Write in advance if you can.
- Write what you want.
- Find your people.
- Guard your writing time fiercely.

8

Always Be Building

"People don't buy what you're doing; they buy why you're doing it."

Simon Sinek

When I was a Realtor, the mantra was "Always be closing," but as a writer, now it's "Always be building." What I mean by that is always be consciously increasing your platform. Your platform is absolutely vital to your success, and you can never neglect it. Every day you must be feeding it, nurturing it, and growing it.

I know this might come as a surprise to some of you, because it would make sense that you should always be writing, right? Well, you need to do that too. You just need to do both. At the same time. I meet many writers who spend an entire year writing a novel and nothing else and then say, "Okay, now I'm ready to work on my platform."

Sorry, pal, you're too late. You needed to be doing that shit daily!

When I travel around the country and speak at writing conferences, I'm often asked, "What does your day look like?"

People imagine me sitting in a cabin in the woods, drinking tea, and writing thousands of words a day that just flow out of me blissfully. They're shocked to hear my real life couldn't be further from the truth. At this point, writing is a j-o-b for me. I have schedules and word count goals that I stick to. I have a list of tasks that need to be done every single day, and at the top of that list is creating content and building my platform.

I work in a windowless basement office and spend just as much time building my platform as I do writing. I work on both throughout the day. I try to post several times a day on my social media platforms. With more than one million people across all the platforms, it can be a full-time job for one person, so the Hubs helps me out. He's really the only person I trust to do it, because he knows my sense of humor the best and he knows my audience very well. He finds content for me to share, he helps me come up with stories to tell, he manages the comments and shields me from a lot of the bullshit on the biggest pages (People I Want to Punch in the Throat, I Just Want to Pee Alone, and You Know It Happens At Your House Too) because he knows I can be dragged into the cesspool of the internet pretty easily. I alone maintain my personal Facebook profile (Jen Mann) and a new one I created (LadyBalls). I also maintain my own Instagram (@piwtpitt). In addition to all this, I have a private Facebook group called No Pants Required. It's a great place to hang out. We mostly talk about books, and we've got a nice community going there. I have two volunteers (Kristin and Gen) who help me out by keeping the conversations going and patrolling for assholes.

Social media can feel like work, and I hear a lot of complaints, but it isn't hard as long as you remember the Golden Rule: be authentic. This is where your readers can get to know you. The real you, or at least as much you as you're willing to share with them. I share entertaining or informative articles. I share funny or empowering memes. I tell stories. I make videos. I share photographs.

Rarely do I ask people to buy my book, though. That is a no-no and this is why: Would you want someone barking, "Buy my book!" all day long? No, you wouldn't. That's annoying AF. Instead, you'd want to connect on a personal level with that author. That's why you need to walk a fine line between being yourself and staying on brand.

For me, my brand is fairly simple: funny stories about me or my family, sweary, books, girl power, elves, rants, weird shit, no pants, and no fucks given. If you don't know what your brand is, ask. Ask your followers, "What are the three things you think of when you think of me?" That will give you a start. The other way to know is to pay attention to your post and track the likes, comments, and shares.

That's how I figured out the no-pants thing. I joke a lot about how much I enjoy working in my pajamas at home and how much I hate getting dressed. There's even an embarrassing story in my book *People I Want to Punch in the Throat: Competitive Crafters, Drop-Off Despots, and Other Suburban Scourges* about getting caught in the school carpool line by the staff in my bunny PJs. Because I rarely get dressed and live in pajamas, I decided one day to snap a photo of myself in real pants. That picture went gangbusters, and I was like, "Hey, you guys really like it when I wear pants. Hmm..." Now I try to take several pictures a month of me in pants.

When I'm sharing on social media, I have my brand identity in the back of my mind. I think twice before I hit share: "Where does this fit? Will it make people laugh? Will it enrage them the way it enraged me? Is it about elves or pants or weird shit?" If I answer yes to any of those questions, I hit share.

If I answer no, I'll pause, and then I still might hit share, because every rule is meant to be broken and sometimes I just want to share what I want to share. For instance, cat videos aren't really part of my brand; it's not something I'm known for and it's not something my audience reacts to in a big way, but I personally love cat videos, so I share cat videos when I'm in the mood. Also, in the last few years I've gotten more political, which is probably a bit of a no-no for authors, but I decided I had a massive platform and I am not happy with what's happening around the world, and if I can shine some light on shit, I will. I figure if I can't use this bullhorn for good, then why have it? Sure, I turn off some people by doing this, but "no fucks given" is also part of my brand, so in a weird branding circle jerk it IS on brand for me to be off-brand. Mind. Blown. Right?

The one rule I follow and never break is: It can't always be about you, dumb-dumb. Yes, people are following you and want to hear from you, but they don't necessarily want to hear *about* you. At least not all the time. I try to keep my posts to the 80/20 rule. Eighty percent of the time I'm posting about other things (but still staying on brand) and twenty percent of the time I'm posting about my products or services.

Unless it's book release day. When it's release day, it's balls-to-wall promotion all day long. I change all my headers, I make my profile pictures the cover of the new book. I never just say, "Buy my book!" I try to always make my sales pitches entertaining or informative for my readers. I share quotes from the book, I share good reviews to encourage sales, and I share bad reviews so we can all laugh together about stupid people who don't get me. I share excerpts. I make videos, I write articles and place them on other sites. I write a blog post; I send out a newsletter. If I could hire a skywriter, I would. I ask my people to help me share.

When I tell writers they must work on their platform daily, they tend to complain about their lack of time. "I work a full-time job. I have a family! My little free time is spent writing, and now you want me to work on social media too?"

YES.

You can't afford not to. I don't care if you're self-published or traditionally published; you're going to be the number one salesman for your book.

But don't worry. It's not as hard as it sounds. Like everything else, it just takes discipline and time-blocking. Remember, I've been in those shoes, so I know how hard it is, but I also know it can be done. When I started writing I was a full-time Realtor, a wife, and a mother of two small children. I didn't know anything about social media. I'd started a Facebook page for my real estate career, but I only shared on it once in a while, and most of my shares were something like, "I need to sell a house this week! Who wants in?" You'll be shocked to know those sorts of updates didn't work, and so I assumed social media was a dud way to market myself.

Because I started my blog as a lark and not as a way to get published, I didn't take social media very seriously. I had a personal Facebook page where I shared adorable photos of my kids and stalked old boyfriends to see if they'd gone bald yet. I wasn't using it wisely, and I definitely wasn't growing it.

Before I went viral, I'd write blog posts and share them with my three hundred friends on my personal Facebook account and that was it. I didn't have a way for people to subscribe to the blog. I didn't have social media accounts dedicated to the blog. I didn't even know that was a thing. When I wrote my Elf on the Shelf post, I did what I always did; I shared it on my personal Facebook account hoping to entertain my readers (most of whom were related to me) and it took off.

When it took off and Ebeneezer told me to get to work, I realized I had a shit-ton of work to do because I was starting from zero. I didn't have any of the tools in place that I should have. One of those tools was a solid platform. Because I'd never studied social media; I didn't know the rules or common practices and instead, I winged it. I ended up being fairly successful and learning as I went along, but imagine how much more successful I could have been if I'd actually been prepared?

When you start writing, you should go ahead and claim all your social media channels. It doesn't matter if you don't have any followers yet. They will come. I'll teach you how to get them. But you want them to be able to find you, and the only way that's going to happen is if you've claimed your name.

What name should you claim?

That's a good question. It really depends on your goals and what you want to be known for. When I started this adventure, I was an anonymous blogger who never revealed my last name or shared a photograph of myself. I didn't want to claim JEN MANN. In my head, Jen Mann was nobody. No one knew Jen Mann. I'd gone viral as **PEOPLE I WANT TO PUNCH IN THE THROAT**, so that was the name I claimed. It worked fine on Facebook, because there wasn't a limit, but when I got to Twitter, I ran into my first problem. The name was way too long to be a Twitter handle. It was also too long for Pinterest. (Instagram and Snapchat didn't exist yet, but it would also be too long for those future platforms.) I didn't know what to do about my handles. There was no way I was sharing my real name, and I didn't make up good fake names when I was under pressure (see Gomer and Adolpha). I'd noticed that some of my readers had taken to abbreviating PEOPLE I WANT TO PUNCH IN THE THROAT to PIWTPITT. I claimed PIWTPITT for Pinterest and @throat_punch for Twitter.

Looking back, it wasn't the wisest decision I made. But it was a decision made completely under the gun and that's what I'm trying to help you avoid. If I'd had more time, I probably would have come up with a suitable pseudonym or a better way to describe myself, because PIWTPITT is weird as hell and tough as nuts. It's not memorable and it's awkward.

Take some time. Figure out what you want to be known as, because if you do this right, those names are going to define you for a long time. You might write science fiction right now and you want to be "SCIFIGUY," but what happens if you change directions in a few years and take up Westerns?

So, for social media only, my recommendation is to always go with your name versus a blog or a series name. Ultimately YOU are your brand. Your readers read you, no matter what you write. It's imperative to have a personal account and then if you want other accounts for your popular blogs or books, do that, but make sure you have a personal account too that will link to all these sub-accounts.

Maybe you write about crafts or recipes and you're like, "But Jen, I'm really known for pies and wreaths! I think my handles should reflect that." I hear you and I understand where you're coming from, but I would argue that Martha Stewart doesn't call herself THE KRAFT QUEEN. Think long and hard before you go with your brand's identity over your own identity.

How You Can F*cking Do It:

- Find your brand.
- Work on your platforms a little bit every day.
- It can't be all about you, dumb-dumb.

9

Just Publish Your Book

"There comes a point in your life when you need to stop reading other people's books and write your own."

Albert Einstein

I don't remember the first time a reader asked me if I was going to write a book, but I do remember my reaction. It was something like, "Seriously?! I'm writing five times a week on the blog, working full-time, and trying to raise kids, and now you want me to write a book? Are you kidding me? When will I do this?"

Yes, I was worried about when I'd write a book, but my real concern was *how* to write a book. Sure, I'd written a lot over the years—for others. And I'd started a lot of my own work, but I'd never actually *finished* anything. Oh, and I had no idea how to get a book published. It was like being five years old all over again and wishing and dreaming to be an author but having no idea how to accomplish my dream.

At this point some of you might be saying, "Wait. You mean New York publishers weren't banging down your door the minute the elf post went viral? Because my neighbor's sister-in-law's cousin shared a video of him braiding his daughter's hair and now he's got an agent and a book deal and they're developing a TV show featuring other dads braiding hair. One guy can even French braid. How did you not get a call?"

I know, right?! It was crazy, but no one called me.

Luckily, the Hubs had a plan. He'd read an article about Amazon's self-publishing arm, CreateSpace, and he felt confident he could publish the book. "You write it, and I'll figure out how to publish it," he said.

I didn't know where to begin. Most blog-to-book creations I'd seen were underwhelming. It was as if the blogger slurped their entire content into a book form—typos, grammatical errors, and all. As a writer I was not impressed with this approach. I thought it looked sloppy and poorly done. As a reader, I really didn't like this idea, because I was not such a fangirl of anyone to pay for content I'd already read for free on the internet.

I knew I needed original content, but I wasn't sure where to begin. Writing five new blog posts a week was already a lot of work, and the idea of coming up with even more seemed like an insane amount of work. Besides the work, I wasn't even sure how to structure a book. Should I write fiction? Nonfiction? What was I supposed to do? I was almost paralyzed by the choices and by my fear of failure.

It was the summer after I'd gone viral and I was at a pool party at my friend Jane's house. She asked me what I was working on.

"I'm trying to write a book," I said.

"What kind of book?" Jane asked.

"That's just it. I have no idea. I'm at a complete loss."

Jane is a marketing executive and gets paid big bucks to help her company see creative ways to package and sell their products. "Is the elf post still your most-read blog post?"

I nodded.

"It will be the one-year anniversary this Christmas, right?"

I nodded.

"So I'd write a hilarious book of other holiday stories and put the elf post in there and build around it."

"What about the fact that so many people have already read it?" I asked.

She shrugged. "So what? It's one post. It's your most famous post. Your super fans will love having a copy of it to read any time you want, and if someone isn't interested, they can skip it. It's just one chapter. The rest will be new original content."

I nodded. Her plan made sense. I liked it a lot. "Okay, I think I can do that," I said. "So, it's June now and I'd need to have the book done by December, right?"

Jane shook her head. "No, you'll miss your selling season if you wait until December. I'd say you need that book on the market by September."

"September?" I squeaked, quickly doing the math. "Holy shit, that's soon."

Jane shrugged again. "I'm just trying to help."

"No, I know. I get it. Fuck. So, I need to start writing..."

"Now?"

"Wrap it up, kids!" I yelled, gathering up beach towels and goggles. "We got to go! Mommy's got a book to write!"

I picked a random date on the calendar as my publication date and started writing that afternoon.

I had no idea how many words a book should be. I didn't break it down and build backward like I do now. I made a list of stories I could tell and I started writing. I changed up my writing process completely. I was still blogging every day and selling real estate full-time and taking care of kids, etc. I didn't have the luxury of just writing a couple hours here and there. I had to get that book done. I wanted it done before the one-year anniversary because I wanted to publish it while my iron was still hot.

One day, the Hubs wandered into my office and asked me if I knew who Stephenie Meyer was.

"No idea," I said.

"She's the author of the *Twilight* series."

"Never heard of it," I said.

"Really? It's a huge bestselling series. The fourth book in the series is coming out and she's doing publicity for it. I watched an interview with her."

"Okay?" I didn't know what he was driving at. I didn't have time to pee; I definitely didn't have time to read a series of books!

"She was talking about her writing process. She's a mom. She's got three kids. She writes books at soccer practice or whatever. She says she's always writing wherever she goes. If she's waiting for the kids, she writes something real quick. She says she finds time all day to write."

"Really?"

"Yeah, I think you should try it. You have a laptop. You could take it with you to swimming lessons or gymnastics and write there while you wait for the kids. You could probably get a lot done."

"I don't know," I said. The idea of hauling my laptop everywhere sounded terrible.

"I'm just saying that's what she does. And you have a deadline looming and that could help you."

Later that day Gomer had a baseball game. We packed up his bat, his glove, his water, and my laptop and off we went. I didn't think I would be able to concentrate with all the noise and distractions, but I managed to bang out a few thousand words and I was hooked. Now I am that mom with my laptop everywhere. I write in the carpool line; I write at soccer, baseball, and basketball games; I write on airplanes. I used to take my kids to indoor play centers at McDonald's and let them run while I wrote. I write at the park; I write at the pool. If I'm meeting someone for lunch or coffee I take my laptop, because there's a chance they're running late and I can knock out some work before they get there. What I'm trying to tell you here is there's no excuse. You can take a notebook or a laptop with you. Put down the book or your phone or whatever you've brought to entertain yourself and get some words on the page. It might feel awkward at first, and people will definitely comment, but do you want to get your book done or not?

About a month from the deadline, the Hubs told me we needed to get a cover designed for the book. He'd done a lot of research and he'd decided on a website called 99designs.com. This is a freelance site where they can design just about anything you can think of. You write a brief about your project and then you run a contest and freelancers submit their work for consideration. Depending upon your requirements, book covers will cost you around five hundred dollars or so.

Never for one second did I consider creating my own cover. I know a lot of self-published authors think this is a great way to cut a corner and save a little money, but we're writers, not designers. Unless you're really skilled at design, I think it's a terrible idea to try and make your own cover.

We all know the saying, "Don't judge a book by its cover," right? That's not true. We all judge a book by its cover. Every day. And if your cover looks like a homemade piece of trash, no one is going to buy that book. Your cover must rock. It must pop off the shelf and catch the eye of everyone walking by. It must stand out in a scrolling sea of thumbnails. I cannot emphasize how important a cover is.

I wrote my brief, and to be honest, it wasn't terrific. I'd never tried to summarize a book, and I was doing a shit job. My details sucked, so the results I got sucked. I was getting worried, because my deadline was coming and I didn't know what I was going to do if I couldn't find a cover.

And then I saw a design that caught my eye. I liked it better than anything else, but it still wasn't right, but I didn't know how to articulate what was wrong. Ben, the designer, sent me an email asking for more guidance. I didn't know what to tell him. Finally he suggested I make a Pinterest board and pin book covers that "spoke" to me. "It can be any genre," he said. "Just pin book covers that stand out to you and give me a brief reason why, if you can."

I went online and starting pinning and after an hour or so I had several to show him.

"I get it," Ben said. "You like bold, clean, irreverent, funny. I can work with this."

He submitted what is still my favorite cover. He got me. He understood me better than I understood myself. I almost cried when I saw that cover, because it was perfection.

I've never had anyone else make me a cover since then. Ben is my guy. I trust him completely, and he's a talented genius. I'm a good writer, but those covers are one of the secrets to my success. My book covers shine. They stop traffic. People comment on them all the time.

I kept writing and the deadline kept getting closer. About a week before the publication date, the Hubs said he needed the manuscript as soon as possible. "Why?" I asked. "I still have another week."

"Yeah, but I need to format it. It has to be all laid out and that looks complicated. It could take me a day or so."

I looked at the bullet list I'd been working from. I still had a couple more stories to write. I could knock them out fairly quickly though. "Okay, I can have it for it by tomorrow."

"Great."

Do you notice anything that we forgot to do?

Yeah, we never hired an editor for this book. It never even crossed my mind. I didn't really consider how important an editor was. I felt like, "I'm a decent writer. I've edited other people. Surely I can edit this book just fine."

That's when I cut a corner and saved a dollar.

That was a stupid thing to do, and I've never done it again. Editors, like cover designers, are worth the investment. You're publishing a book that you want to sell to people. You're giving them a product. Don't you want it to be the highest quality product you can offer? There's a shit-ton of competition out there, and you don't want to be known as the author who puts out an inferior book.

You have to spend money to make money. Are you worth the investment or not?

Editors can be hard to find, though, because anyone who is any good is usually quite busy and doesn't have room to take on a new client. Trust me, though, there are plenty of great editors out there; you just have to do some work to find them. Ask other writers for referrals, read the acknowledgments in books you like, go to conferences, do a Google search.

I have several freelance editors I work with. They each specialize in different genres, so depending upon the book, I get on a certain editor's schedule. You can't just contact an editor a week or two before you want the work done. My editors are in high-demand, so I'm usually booking them four to eight months in advance. This is why I set my publishing schedule for the year in advance and I know what my deadlines are based on my editors' schedules as well as Ben's. Sometimes I have Ben making me covers way in advance because I know he'll be busy close to my release date. I already know what the book is going to be about, so picking a cover in advance isn't such a big deal.

Another mistake I made was I didn't do any research into how long a book should be. A standard nonfiction book should be at least fifty thousand words. A fiction novel for adults should be at least sixty thousand words. The first version of *Spending the Holidays with People I Want to Punch in the Throat* only ended up being about forty thousand words, but it felt like a hundred thousand when I was finished.

At that point I didn't care, and I didn't think I had time to make any changes. My publication date was coming fast and the Hubs was struggling to get the book formatted. There are many services out there that will format your book for a fee, but again, we were trying to do this as cheaply as possible, so we thought we could save some money and do it ourselves.

The thing about formatting is when you're creating a physical book, every single thing you see on that page must be put there. So he had to put every header and every page number on there. He had to choose where to break a page. He had to figure out how to make each chapter start on a facing page instead of the back of another page. It was time-consuming and so frustrating. I think it took him four whole days of cussing and irritation before he finally got it done. It wasn't perfect, but it was good enough.

Over the years, the Hubs created a template for himself to use for future books. When he used his template it would only take him a day to format a book. But I still wasn't pleased with his work. I wanted my books to look better, so I hired an outside company to do at least one, maybe two of the books. And then I heard about Vellum.

Vellum is a game-changer. It's not cheap and you need a Mac, but it's ah-may-zing. I've taken over formatting, and it takes me a couple hours now to get a gorgeous-looking book. I can't recommend this product enough.

Once *Spending the Holidays with People I Want to Punch in the Throat* was formatted, it was time to hit publish. We bought an ISBN number and uploaded the files. I always upload directly to Amazon because they sell the bulk of my books, and I like to keep those numbers separate. Even though Amazon sells the most, I still publish all my books wide. This means they can be found on every platform out there. I think that's important, because I don't want to put all my eggs in one basket. When one site controls all the content, that's not good for anyone.

I use Draft2Digital to upload to the other sites. Draft2Digital takes an additional percentage, but it's worth not having to upload everywhere individually. You don't get an advance when you self-publish, but it also costs nothing to upload your book to these sites. Everybody gets paid when the book sells.

We hit publish across the board and then I went on social media and my blog and told everyone my new book was available. That was all it took back then, because my status updates were shared easily and the platforms weren't throttling my reach. Also, it helped that it was my very book. I was right to want to get it done quickly, because my fanbase was still quite excited about me. The book was highly anticipated and it went to top of charts on Amazon.

I sold a shit-ton of books that first week, but I did not hit the *New York Times* bestseller list. I wasn't very surprised at the time, because I didn't know much about the list and how it all worked. There's a lot of mystery behind that list, and no one knows the exact formula it takes to garner a spot. After years of research I've come up with IT DEPENDS.

A lot of factors go into hitting that list, and one of them was back in 2012 they only counted traditionally published book sales. This was a real issue with indie authors, because there were a lot of people selling a lot of books and not being recognized for their accomplishment. Knowing what I know now, I think I probably had a shot at hitting the list, but again, IT DEPENDS.

It depends on what the competition looked like that exact week. When you release a book with the intent to hit the list, you're competing with everything else that's selling that week. So, one author might hit the list with only five thousand books sold, but another author during another week might need to sell fifteen thousand to nab the same spot.

This is where it's kind of nice to have an agent or an editor on the inside, because they know which weeks are historically low sales weeks and they can advise you. For instance, I had a friend who was told Labor Day weekend is a slow time of year. So, that week she dropped her e-book down to ninety-nine cents and paid several different sites to advertise the price to their subscribers. She called in every favor from everyone she knew, and then she said a little prayer. It paid off and she hit the list. The next year another friend of mine tried to copy the same plan and she missed it completely. You just have no idea.

How You Can F*cking Do It:

- Don't be deterred by hard work.
- Figure out what you don't know.
- Don't be afraid to ask for help.

10

Make Some Friends

"Find a group of people that challenge and inspire you. Spend a lot of time with them and it will change your life."

Amy Poehler

Tribe, club, clique, posse, gang, squad, whatever you want to call them. You need one. Stop what you're doing and go get one right now. Well, not right now, but when you're done with this book, make that a priority because this whole writing thing is a lonely-ass business and you're going to need some support.

I'm not talking about your real-life friends. Those people are probably really, really fine, but I'm talking about an online group. I'm talking about a passel of penmen who understand your struggle to fill a blank page and will cheer you on when you're rocking the keyboard or commiserate with you when you're blocked. I'm talking about a bevy of beauties who will stroke your hair and tell you people are idiots when you get a bad review or troll sending you hate mail. I'm talking about a gaggle of gospelers who will sing your praises and lift you up and tell the world about you.

I'm sure you've figured out by now that my husband is great and all, but he's not a writer. He doesn't understand staring at a wall for thirty minutes totally counts as "working" or my overwhelming desire to dissect every one-star review. He doesn't understand how it feels to push "publish" on something so personal and vulnerable that you cried the whole time you wrote it. He doesn't understand the elation you get when someone tells them your words made their day or helped them get through a rough time in their life. He doesn't understand the feeling of pure elation when someone says you made them laugh so hard they spit out their drink. He just doesn't get it. Like, at all.

A lot of writers feel like other writers are their competition or their enemy. I get that. When I was in real estate, I didn't make friends with other Realtors. We weren't hanging out and being besties, because we were literally competing for the same clients. A person only moves so many times in their life and I wanted them to pick me to be their Realtor every single time, not my good friend, Joan!

But readers are different. Readers are voracious. They don't follow just one author or even one genre. Put on your reader hat for a moment and think about your bookshelf. How many of those authors are your "favorite"? How many of them would you love to meet and get a book signed by? How many authors do you recommend to your friends? How many genres do you read?

Tons, right?

That's why writers aren't your competition. I mean,

there's always an asshole in the bunch who acts that way, but we're not talking about him.

To be honest, I didn't see it that way at first. When the Elf on the Shelf post went viral, I really freaked the freak out and went deep underground. Not only was I afraid to talk to readers, I was very leery of the writers who reached out to me as well. I felt like a lot of them wanted something from me. I got tons of emails from other bloggers who wanted to be my BFF as long as I'd pimp out their work to my readers. I had lots of offers from other writers to write guest posts for my blog so they could expand their own readership. I didn't respond to any of these emails because they approached me the wrong way. I still don't know what their motivation was, but their introductions were all wrong.

When you're trying to make friends with someone and form a bond, you have to show them what you can do for them, not vice versa. (Remember, it's not always about you, dumb-dumb.) That's how I met the first person in my girl gang: Robin O'Bryant. Because Robin approached me the right way. I could tell she'd done her research and gone back into my archives to read my stuff and really figured out who I was. Instead of being like so many people who wrote me and said, "I'm hilarious" with nothing to back up that statement, Robin let her funny personality come through the email. She didn't have to assure me she was hilarious, she *showed* me she was hilarious. And she didn't ask for anything except my mailing address. She'd written and published a funny book and she thought I might enjoy reading it and she wanted to send me a copy. She didn't ask for a review or a shout-out on social media. She just said I'd entertained her and now she'd like to return the favor.

When her book arrived I was swamped and it sat on my desk for weeks. When I finally cracked it open and read it, I realized she was my long-lost best friend, sister, and soul mate all wrapped into one person. I quickly emailed her back hoping she hadn't forgotten me. Luckily she hadn't and we developed an instant friendship.

Robin was an experienced writer and blogger and she taught me that she wasn't my competition. It was better if we worked together, because we could share an audience. If someone liked me, they'd love Robin. When I told her I was working on a self-published book, she gave me so many pointers about selling books and speaking to audiences. She also helped me learn how to interact with my fans. Up until that point, I'd been keeping them at arm's length, and I was very closed off and didn't interact with them very much. It wasn't because I didn't want to; it was because I didn't know how to. I didn't have the confidence or knowledge I needed.

I remember some of the first words of advice Robin gave me. It was about my response to her email. "You didn't ask me for a recommendation," she said.

"What are you talking about?" I asked.

"When I emailed you the first time and told you that I thought you were hysterical, your response should have been, 'Thanks so much, please do me a favor and tell a friend about me!'"

I immediately felt queasy. "No way. I could never do that."

"Why not?"

"It just isn't me. I can't do that. What if they said no? I'd be mortified."

"That's the thing, Jen. Those aren't the people who are going to say no," she said. "Don't you get it? If they went to the trouble to track down your email address and send you a note saying how great you are, you think they won't tell someone else if you ask them?"

"I guess I just thought if they liked it, they'd tell someone."

"Not always. That's why you have to ask, because when you ask, it puts the idea in their head."

"I didn't think about it that way," I admitted.

"When people tell me they love my book, I thank them and then I ask for a review on Amazon. I tell them they could copy and paste the email they sent me. Drop it in Amazon and put five stars on it, done and done. They like you, Jen. They wouldn't write you and say they liked you if they didn't."

"I guess so," I said.

"Trust me," she said. "Try it next time. You'll see."

So the next time I received an email from a fan, I took a big gulp and I asked for a recommendation. "Thank you so much for the email," I wrote. "I appreciate it so much and I'm so glad to hear I entertained you. Would you do me a giant favor and share that post with a friend?"

To my immense surprise, the response was, "Of course!"

After that I started asking for reviews and recommendations every time. And Robin was right, very rarely did anyone turn me down.

Robin also introduced me to my Girl Gang—some of the best women on the internet. We're spread out all over the country, so we only get to hang out online with the occasional retreat somewhere (never Kansas, those assholes). We're all at different points in our writing careers. We all have different goals. We're all on our own paths to success. But we support one another through it all. We cross-promote one another, we collaborate on projects, we brainstorm together, and we share one another's work whenever we can. We talk all day, every day, and we've seen some *shit*. We've been through the career (and personal) highs and lows with one another and we trust one another completely. We have each other's backs.

We are open and honest with one another about our successes and our struggles. We share job opportunities and we cheer one another on. When I travel around the country to speak, these ladies drive hours to show up and support me. They let me crash in their guest rooms, they feed me and shuttle me around.

My Girl Gang isn't a secret, but it is private. Sometimes other writers will tell me they're jealous, and I get that. It can hurt to feel excluded, but I assure you, it's nothing personal when people form these tight-knit groups and then close the door. Because we are so deeply connected and vulnerable and honest with what we share with one another, we can't imagine bringing anyone else into the fold at this point.

That shouldn't stop you from creating your own Gang. Look around and see who you fit with and invite them to join your group. It's actually better to be in charge, because then you will most certainly like everyone in the group if nothing else. Don't worry so much about people's levels of success, but rather are they givers or takers. You want your gang to be a group of givers or else it's not going to work.

Besides my Girl Gang, I also have lots of other tribes. I've joined several online groups for bloggers, nonfiction writers, humor writers, young adult writers, moms who write, parents who write, women writers. You name it, I've got a group for it. Most of these groups are very big and they're not as exclusive as my Girl Gang.

I have found, over the years, that you get back what you put into the group. I'm quite active in some groups, and I get a lot of return on my investment. I'm given a lot of support and offered opportunities. I'm known as an expert on a lot of topics, so I'm recommended or sought out. I've made a lot of friends in those groups, and that's where I find a lot of writers to work with me on my anthologies and other collaborations. I'm a lurker in other groups. I don't feel comfortable talking in those groups, not because I'm being a taker, but more because I feel completely out of my league. I don't feel like I have anything I can teach those people and I feel lucky just to be able to sit at their feet and learn. To give back, I try to share their work or refer my friends to them, but that's really all I can offer.

I find out about these groups either through person meetings at conferences, networking groups, professional writing organizations, private invitation, word of mouth, or searches on social media.

Not only do you need a tribe, you also need strategic alliances. Strategic alliances are different, because it's a professional relationship. You might make friends with some of your alliances, but it's not the same. Alliances are all about tit-for-tat, reach-arounds, win-win, and so on. We're not pairing up to be pals; we're joining forces to conquer together. My first strategic alliance became my friend, but that's a rarity.

The publishing world was a different place back then in 2012. They kind of turned their noses up at the internet viral sensations and didn't consider blogging to be writing. They hadn't realized yet that we could sell a shit-ton of books; they were still focused on the fact that I used "fuck" as often as possible, and that wasn't literary.

I didn't get a call from news channels or agents or anyone. The only person who reached out to me was Farah Miller, the editor of the Parenting section at Huffington Post.

In those days HuffPo was the place to be. They had a massive audience and a great reputation. If you were a blogger, especially a parenting and/or humor blogger, you wanted your content on HuffPost, but I didn't know that because I was a dumbass. I was still looking at other bloggers as my enemies, not my partners.

When Farah contacted me the Elf on the Shelf was about two days into its viral run. We'd had the big spike and it had dropped, but it was still being read quite a bit. Farah emailed me and asked me if she could run my Elf on the Shelf post on the Parenting page of HuffPo. I made one of the biggest mistakes I've made along the way. I said, "No." I said no because I didn't understand what cross-promotion could do for me. I couldn't see the big picture. I was still so naive and caught up in my own ego and my own paranoia. I felt like if I allowed HuffPo to run my Elf post, I'd "lose" those readers. What I didn't understand was that by allowing HuffPo access, I'd actually find more readers. Those readers were never going to find me any other way. I needed HuffPost's readership. If I'd allowed them to run the Elf, I bet it would have gone super-viral and everything would have gone differently. Editors and agents read the HuffPost, and maybe someone might have read it and taken a chance on me. Maybe I would have been offered a television deal or a full-time writing gig at another site. Who knows? We'll never know, because I said, "No."

I was also a bit irritated because HuffPo didn't pay their contributors. If you've ever heard me speak or talked to me about writing, one thing I'm adamant about is getting paid. We are content creators and content is king. Publishers make money off our words, so it makes me cringe when I see people give away their words for free. Nothing irritates me more than when a huge, well-known brand asks me to write a post about their product in return for "exposure." Exposure doesn't pay my fucking bills.

When I want something from this huge brand, I don't say, "You should give it to me for free and I'll guarantee you exposure." They'd laugh in my face and so should writers.

BUT.

There's always a but, isn't there?

There will be a time or two when it will behoove you to write for exposure. Yes, you want to be paid and yes, you should be paid, but sometimes there are things we all do for free, because we know that down the road it will lead to more paying opportunities. And now that I have books I can sell, I tend to do stuff in exchange for book sales. For instance, I'll speak at civic groups and book clubs and writer's clubs for free as long as they allow me to sell books when I'm done. I know that I'll give a great speech and that will motivate people to buy my books.

HuffPo was one of those times. It irked me they didn't pay, but I couldn't pass up the opportunity of getting my work in front of all those eyeballs. I knew that much, at least.

I could tell Farah was frustrated with me, but she couldn't get through to me. Luckily, she didn't give up on me, though. She suggested I write something else for them.

I like to think of myself as a storyteller, but I could see that lists were very popular on HuffPo and other sites like it. I wanted to write something that would have legs and that would lure people to me, but I also had to write for their audience. The idea is that I'm never going to get all of them, but I'm always trying to peel off "my people" from the masses. I knew if I wrote a funny, snarky, sassy list, I'd entertain HuffPo's readers and I'd find my people.

I put together what I thought was a no-brainer list. It was sarcastic and biting with a hint of love—my signature style. I thought the list would be a big hit and I'd find millions of people to follow me.

Instead, I was introduced to the world of internet trolls.

When I went viral on my own site, I'd had what I thought were trolls stop by and give me a piece of their mind, but it wasn't until my first outing on HuffPo that I realized trolls weren't just kind of nuts, they were also total fucking assholes who make it their missions in life to drive you to suicide.

These motherfuckers came out of the woodwork and started destroying me in the comments section. It was clear they didn't get my sense of humor and they weren't entertained by me. At. All.

I emailed Farah to complain that her readers had no sense of humor. "It's satire!" I wrote. "How can they not see that?"

Farah, bless her, tried to smooth my hair and assure me I was still pretty. She talked me down off the ledge and explained to me, "You. Never. Read. The. Comments. EVER."

I'd always read my comments. How else would I know if people liked what I was writing? I liked to talk to my readers and, I'll admit, sometimes I liked to poke the bear and tell people to go fuck themselves.

The list I wrote for HuffPo was a decent hit, and it started a long and fruitful relationship with Farah and her team. I found that HuffPo was a great place to throw more gasoline on fires I started.

I'd write a blog post that would catch on with my own audience and then when it started to die down, I'd repost it on HuffPo and let them blow it up again. I found thousands of followers this way. And because I cultivated relationships with her team, I was always on their minds when they were putting together roundups. They loved to do "funniest moms" or "best parenting posts of the week," and I was always someone they at least looked at. I didn't make all the lists, but I made a bunch of them, and those lists and reposts led to other opportunities. Just as I'd hoped.

I was hired on as a freelancer for Babble, another large parenting site. I was there for a few months, but I never really fit in. It had nothing to do with the staff or even the other freelancers. It was me. It made me realize I really didn't like freelancing. I love writing, but I hate writing what other people tell me to write. I love writing, but I kind of hate hard deadlines. I love writing, but I hate sap. Most parenting sites want sap. That's what "sells" for them. They like the heartwarming shit that makes me want to vomit. They also loooooove lists. I'd done a list for HuffPo the first time, but I really shied away after that. I felt like lists encouraged stupidity. If you can't focus long enough to read a four-hundred-word essay, then I weep for you. Lists were the lowest common denominator of content, and I hated them. But Babble loved them.

I had a lot of freedom at Babble. I had a weekly number of posts they wanted from me, and I'd upload them myself without any editorial oversight. One day my editor realized she'd probably made a mistake letting me run free.

There were several freelancers, and if you had an idea you wanted to write about, you'd "claim" it on a group chat so no one else would do it. I was getting frustrated because the other writers would claim things like, "Moms at Christmas!" and "Parenting preschoolers!"

What the fuck? Those are some seriously broad terms and now they're completely off-limits for the rest of us? Really?

It was deadline day and I didn't have anything good to write about because I felt like everything I wanted to write about was "claimed." I started getting mad, and I could feel the anger boiling up inside me, and I sat down at my computer, because I do some of my best shit when I'm pissed.

I banged out a list and put it up on the site with minutes to spare. I saw it post and I watched it for a few minutes. (I always watch my posts for the first few minutes so I can get a feel for how it's going to do.) It started to get comments, likes, and shares almost immediately.

A couple hours later I checked on it again to see how it was doing. I was surprised (sort of) to find it missing from the site. I found an email from my editor. She probably should have chewed me out, but she was very professional and calm when she explained she didn't think having a list called "Top 10 Reasons Moms Read Lists" was a good fit for the site. Especially when number one is: "You're a moron." She went on to suggest some ways we could work together to tone down the message of the list and to make it more appealing and friendly.

I don't think I quit that day, but I know I quit soon after.

Like I said, it wasn't them; it was me. But I'd learned my lesson, so I knew better when NickMoms came calling. NickMoms was a huge humor site, and they walked the snark line a lot closer than Babble. They were a much better fit for me. But I'd realized I didn't like freelancing. I didn't want to be tied down like that. I didn't feel like selling original content for a few dollars and losing all control and ownership of my work. So instead I created a partnership with NickMoms.

In those days I was making quite a bit of ad revenue from my blog, and I wanted more eyeballs. I knew if I could get their readers to my site, they'd stay and read and probably buy some books.

I formed a sharing agreement with NickMoms where

we guaranteed one another a certain number of pageviews every month. Sometimes it would take one post to reach our goal and sometimes it would take five posts. You never knew. We put tracking IDs on the posts so we could both keep track, and we both felt like it was a win-win for us.

I used this same approach with many sites over the years and was usually happy with the results. Every now and again you partner with someone who doesn't uphold their end of the bargain, but that's rare.

How You Can F*cking Do It:

- Be brave.
- Be sincere.
- Put yourself out there.

11

Get Yourself a Hype Man

"Opportunities don't happen, you create them."

Chriis Grosser

It is really awkward to brag about yourself, so you need a third party to do that for you. You need a hype man/woman/person to get people excited about you. It's always so much better when someone else is doing the talking about you and you can just stand there and look humble.

Believe it or not, I haven't always been the ball of fire and fury and confidence I am today. I've gotten a lot better over the years, but at the beginning of this adventure I was a meek, quiet little thing. I was very shy and uncomfortable to have any attention on me.

That's why it's a good thing I have a hype man for a husband. The Hubs is so good at hype that it can be embarrassing sometimes. However, this is exactly what I need.

When I'm lacking confidence or having a shit day and feeling particularly attacked, it's nice to have someone there to hold my hand and assure me that I'm a goddamn genius. It's nice to have someone say, "Fuck the haters, now get back to work, Jen." It's nice to have someone point out the positive comments, reviews, and emails and remind me why I'm doing this.

Being a writer is a very fragile business. It's fucked up, really, when you think about it. We're usually damaged people (especially if you're a funny writer, there's some dark shit in your past that's made you so funny), and we aren't usually known for our incredible sense of self-worth. We put our deepest, darkest thoughts out there on the page and hope people respond appropriately. There aren't a lot of jobs where your daily feedback is "Go kill yourself" or "You suck." And yet, we still keep at it. What is that all about? (Actually, that's probably a whole other book!)

And it doesn't even need to be such harsh criticism to make a writer doubt herself. When I was working on the promotional material for *People I Want to Punch in the Throat*, I kept describing myself as "hysterical," and my team at Penguin Random House kept changing it to "funny." It really rubbed me the wrong way. It was a such a subtle thing, but words matter, especially when you're a writer. It was like they were saying, "Easy, killer, you're not *that* funny."

When I showed the Hubs, I was like, "Fuck that, I'm hysterical and I have a billion emails from readers to prove it! Right????"

And he was like, "One hundred percent." Because that's what a good hype man does.

A good hype man understands your goals and he's always working toward helping you accomplish them.

For instance, when we self-published *Spending the Holidays with People I Want to Punch in the Throat* and it went to the top of the Amazon sales charts, the Hubs asked me, "Okay, what do you want now?"

Yes, the book had been successful, but people still gave me that "look" when I said it was self-published. They acted like maybe I self-published because I couldn't get an agent or a traditional publishing deal. I hated that look, and I hated how it made me feel. Deep down, I knew my ego wouldn't let me feel successful until I had a traditional-publishing deal. It's stupid, I know, but there's no sense arguing with your ego. You're never going to win.

"I want to see my book in a brick-and-mortar bookstore," I said. "I want to land an agent, a traditional-publishing deal, and a spot on the *New York Times* best-seller's list."

The Hubs nodded. "All right, let's do it."

A few weeks later, an opportunity presented itself.

Jeff Kinney, the wildly successful author of the *Diary of a Wimpy Kid* series was coming to Kansas City to kick off a cross-country tour for his latest book. As a "popular local blogger," somehow yours truly got on the guest list. That's right. I received an email inviting me to a private meet-and-greet session with Jeff where we could ask questions, take pictures, and get his autograph. I about crapped my pants. Then I told Gomer and he about crapped his.

I realize I have a whole chapter in this book about boundaries and separating my online world from my real world and how the two shall never meet, but for this, I was willing to make an exception. At the time my kids were huge fans of Jeff Kinney's and I knew they'd lose their minds if I took them to meet him.

Since I use F-bombs like commas, I am not what brands would consider "family friendly." I rarely get invited to anything for kids and the fact that I was invited to this was really kind of nuts. This was the universe conspiring FOR me. It had to be. It was the only logical explanation.

I kept waiting for someone to contact me and tell me there had been a horrible mistake and I was no longer invited. I replied before someone realized I'd been invited by mistake and the invitation was rescinded.

I will be there! And I'll be on my best behavior!

Before I meet someone like a Jeff Kinney, I do my research. You have to. You can't walk into a meeting cold. You need to know everything you can, and with the internet at your fingertips, you have no excuse. I, of course, knew of his books (I'd bought several copies over the years and read and reread them with my kids), but I didn't know much about his background. How he got started. What else he was working on, that sort of thing.

I read everything I could and I listened to a few podcasts and radio interviews with him. The morning of the event I sat down to listen to him being interviewed on my favorite radio station, KCUR. What an amazing story Jeff Kinney has! Let me just give you the short version of what I learned: He had a popular website where he'd feature his Wimpy Kid stories. In the meantime, he worked on his manuscript for the first *Diary of a Wimpy Kid* book for almost eight years and then finally he went to Comicon and met a publisher. He showed the publisher his work and immediately he signed Jeff up and they put out the first book. It hit the *New York Times* bestseller list and stayed there for basically forever. Even though Jeff

Kinney has sold over one hundred fifty million copies of his books, he kept his day job as an online game developer and designer for years. This really surprised me, because I'd had one mildly successful book and I was ready to jump into writing full-time. Listening to him gave me pause and made me reconsider. I wouldn't quit my day job for several more years thanks to Jeff Kinney's advice.

One of the points Jeff made during his interview was that he always says yes to a book purchase because it encourages a love of reading in his sons. I couldn't agree more—that's why Gomer owned all the *Wimpy Kid* books.

I had to let Jeff know Gomer was his biggest fan, so I tweeted KCUR while he was being interviewed, and because I'd already been interviewed on the same show, the producers knew my Twitter handle and read my tweet on-air. Jeff reacted the way a normal person does when they get a tweet from someone called @throat_punch. He laughed, but also got a little nervous I was going to punch him in the throat. I assured him I was just the mother of his two biggest fans and we were excited to meet him.

That afternoon we pulled the kids out of school early and headed to the Wimpy Kid event. We were almost there when the Hubs handed me a couple copies of *Spending the Holidays with People I Want to Punch in the Throat*. "Here," he said. "Sign these."

"Who are they for?" I asked, pulling a Sharpie from my purse. (Yes, I always keep a Sharpie in my purse. You never know when someone might want you to scribble in their book.)

"Jeff Kinney and his publicist, Rick."

"Wait. What?" I screeched. "What are you doing?"

"I have a plan. We're going to get your book in their hands. His publicist will go back to New York with your book, and that's what's going to get you a traditional book deal."

"I can't do that!" I said. I was more than a little upset, because there is a code. A set of rules and manners people follow. And ambushing someone at a book signing with your book is simply not done in polite circles.

But the Hubs isn't polite. The Hubs is a hype man. He gets shit done, any way he can. "Sign the books," he ordered. "I'll take care of the rest. You can just stand there if you want."

And that's exactly how it went.

When we arrived at the event, the mom bloggers who were invited to the meet-and-greet were ushered onto Jeff Kinney's tour bus. We were all a little star-struck, and we stood there staring at the poor man while our kids scratched their butts and picked their noses. Finally he broke the silence. "Sooo, what do you all write?" he asked. "What are the names of your blogs?"

No one said anything. The silence was deafening. I wasn't very brave back then, but I hated silence more than I hated being on display, so I spoke up to fill the void. "People I Want to Punch in the Throat," I said a little too loudly.

Rick looked concerned.

Two moms gasped. But in a good way. "I. Love. You," one of them said.

Now Rick looked intrigued.

I was surprised. I really hadn't received public accolades before, and I wasn't sure how to react, so I made it real awkward when I kind of mumbled, "Oh, thanks. Good. You?"

The Hubs piped up, "She writes books too, Mr. Kinney!"

"Oh yeah?" Jeff replied with more kindness than was

warranted. We were hijacking his event, and I was mortified.

Rick's phone rang and he stepped off the bus.

The Hubs watched him go and then gave me the thumbs up. "I'm going in," he whispered. He got off the bus and left me in charge of getting the kids' book signed. I mumble/slurred a few more words in Jeff Kinney's direction and then herded my kids off the bus. We found the Hubs on the sidewalk deep in conversation with Rick.

"Here she is!" the Hubs announced.

"Hello," I said, shaking Rick's hand.

"I'm telling you, my wife is super talented and she's got this book," the Hubs handed Rick a copy of *Spending the Holidays with People I Want to Punch in the Throat*. Rick glanced at it while the Hubs kept talking, "It's a huge bestseller. It's at the top of the charts on Amazon. And it's kicking your butt."

Rick's head swiveled in my direction.

"Not *Wimpy Kid*," I said quickly. "We could never beat *Wimpy Kid*."

The Hubs shook his head. "You don't know that, Jen."

My face was on fire. "It's another one of your titles. A funny mom book. We're beating that one," I said.

"How do you know you're beating it?" Rick asked.

"Because we're self-published. I can see Jen's sales numbers updated hourly. I can also see our ranking compared to other books in her category. We're always ahead of your book, which tells me we're selling more copies than you are."

"Through Amazon," Rick clarified.

The Hubs shrugged. "Yeah, but we all know they sell the bulk of the books."

That was when Rick was told it was time to start the book signing. He gave me his business card and thanked us for the books and said he'd make sure Jeff got his signed copy.

As he walked away, the Hubs got in one last pitch, "This is book is just the beginning! Jen's already got another one ready to go!"

I almost punched him in the throat. I was still recovering from writing that book. I didn't have any other ideas! "Shut up!" I hissed. "I do not! What if he asks to see what I have?"

Ebeneezer blew off my concerns. "Eh, don't worry about it. You can whip up something real fast if you have to!"

It had taken every bit of time, energy, and focus to write that one book. There was no way I could do that again right away! I decided not to worry about it, because I really thought that would be the end.

A few weeks later the Hubs asked me if I'd heard from Rick or anyone else at the publishing house. When I told him no, he said I needed to send an email and follow up with him. "If he was interested in the book, he would have called me already," I argued.

"That's not true," Ebeneezer said. "You have no idea what's going on. You need to touch base and goose him a bit. See what he thinks. At least get some feedback."

Frankly, I was a bit terrified to get feedback. What if he hated it? What if he came back and said it was utter shit and he couldn't believe anyone had bought it? I pushed down the fear and sent him an email to check in.

He sent back a very nice reply. He said he and Jeff had been traveling for weeks on the bus. They'd received all kinds of gifts (including my books) and every night the bus driver would clean the bus and throw everything in the trash. My first thought was for all those adorable pictures of Greg every super-fan probably drew hitting the garbage can; my second thought was for my book baby. Rick was sorry to say that my books most likely ended up in the dustbin.

NOOOOOOOOOOOOOOOOOOO!

However! He told me he was back in the office and he promised if I sent another copy he would make sure someone in the office read it and gave me some feedback.

You guys, that was HUGE. I don't think you understand what a gift that was. Most writers end up in a black hole and never hear back. The fact that he replied and offered to read the book was amazing.

I didn't mess around or fret, I just boxed up a couple more copies of the book and overnighted them to him before he forgot his promise.

Within a couple weeks I had an email from Sarah, an editor, asking to set up a phone call.

The day of the call came and I had a very nice conversation with Sarah. She asked about my sales. "How many books have you sold?"

"Around fifteen thousand copies," I said.

"Didn't the book come out a few months ago?" she asked, surprised.

"Yes. Is that a lot of books?" I asked innocently. But I knew it was. I knew fifteen thousand books in a couple of months was impressive, but I acted like I was clueless.

Sarah didn't let on she was impressed. She said casually, "It's a good amount."

Good amount! Bullshit. *Publishers Weekly* says the average book sells three thousand copies in its lifetime. I'd sold five times that in the first few months.

"How did you sell so many?" she asked. "How did you get the word out?"

I wanted to say, "I wrote a fucking funny book!" But instead I said, "Social media and my blog. I told my readers about it and they bought and then they liked it and told their friends."

"You have a lot of reviews," she said.

"A few hundred," I said.

"Yeah, how did you get so many reviews?"

"I asked for them," I said. "Every time someone told me they enjoyed the book I asked them to leave me a review. I also put a request at the end of the book. I asked readers to leave me a review right then as soon as they were finished reading."

"Interesting," she said.

"People will help you if you ask," I said.

"That's great. Well, I understand your husband told Rick you have another book," she said. "I'd like to take a look at that one, please."

FUUUUUUUUCKKKKKK! I knew that was going to bite me in the ass! I had to think fast. "Umm, well, it's just that it's in really rough shape and I'm not really ready for anyone to take a look at it..." Hey, I wasn't lying. Because it was just an idea in my head, it *was* really rough and not ready for anyone to see yet.

"I understand. I just wanted to get a feel for it. I love your voice, and I think we could work together, but I'd want to see the new book. Maybe you have a few chapters you could show me?"

DAMN IT!! "Yeah, I don't know. I don't really work like that. My chapters are really sparse and then I fill in with the details..." That also wasn't a lie. That's really how I write. I sort of vomit the basics of the story onto the page and then I got back over it a few times filling in the backstory, adding details and humor.

She sighed. "Okay, how about a working title and a table of contents?" she asked.

I thought about it. I had been contemplating a new

book and I could probably come up with a title pretty fast. A table of contents, though? Hmm, that might be harder. But maybe not, I realized. When I write a nonfiction book I work from a bullet list of stories I want to tell, and since I scheduled the call with Sarah, I'd been working on a list of stories for the next book. I could fix it up and make that a loose table of contents. "Sure, I can do that," I said.

"Great!" she replied. "Email it to me when you get a chance."

I came up with a working title and put together a list of stories I could tell. I wrote brief paragraphs for each bullet point explaining a bit of the story. I made sure every story I was telling was an original story and couldn't be found anywhere else. This is something I've always tried to do. I hate nothing more than when a blogger slurps her blog into a book. Bitch, I already read that stuff for free, and now you want me to buy it? Sure, I might revisit the same popular or general topics (like PTA drama or raising spoiled kids), but I won't repeat a story. I don't need to; I kind find humor in everything I do. If I need fodder, I just leave my house and something will inevitably happen to me.

After I sent it over, Sarah and I had another call. That's when she told me she was interested in my new book, but she had some advice for me. "You really need to get an agent," she said.

"I do?" I asked.

"Yes. I could make you an offer and we could get a deal put together, but you should be represented. You need to protect yourself."

Sarah was a giver that day. I was ready to make a deal. I would have probably accepted whatever she offered. I'm sure her offer would have been a respectable offer, but it would not have been near the six-figures that I managed to get. I know this for a fact, because a couple years ago I met a local author for coffee. He was another internet sensation who had landed a book deal. A publisher had come to him and offered him a deal. He was unrepresented, and he didn't think he needed to have an agent. He felt honored to even receive what he did. I asked him point blank what his advance was. When he told me, I almost spit out my tea, and not because it was impressive. Dude got hosed. He was worth three or four times that, and I told him so. I gave him name and contact information of an agent I'd met. She wasn't a good fit for me, but she was a perfect fit for him.

Right after his second book came out I happened to be seated next to his editor on a publishing panel. I introduced myself and he said, "Yes, I know who you are. You cost me a lot of money." He was teasing but not really, you know?

I laughed. "Oh yeah?" I said. "How so?"

"You introduced Daniel to his agent, and she negotiated his book deal."

I smiled. "And?"

"And he got a lot more money." The editor kind of scowled.

"I would say he got what he was worth. You'll be fine. You'll make your investment back," I said.

And that is why you need an agent, folks! But I still hadn't figured that out yet. I know Sarah recommended it, and I should have hopped to, but I'm a person who sort of ruminates on work that needs to be done, and I like to put it off as long as possible until I feel like I have a fully formulated plan. I got off the phone with Sarah and jumped in the bathtub. You might think this is weird, but I do my best thinking in the shower and the bathtub (that's why I order Aqua Notes in bulk). I was in there soaking and trying to figure out the best way to attack querying agents when the Hubs came in carrying his laptop.

"Hey," he said.

"Hey," I said. "I'm naked for thinking, not for you." (Hey, I like to set clear boundaries with everyone.)

"Yeah, yeah, I know," he said. "Listen, I went ahead and queried some agents for you."

I about broke my damn leg jumping out of that bathtub. "Oh my god, Ebeneezer! Are you fucking kidding me?" I screamed. "What the fuck are you doing? You're going to ruin everything!"

The Hubs actually looked quite calm considering a slippery naked woman was coming for this throat. "Relax, I'm helping you," he said.

"There is a process to querying! An art even!" I yelled, grabbing a towel. "Each agent has their own thing. You have to read their requirements. You have to do it just right or else you'll get tossed! You only get one shot with these people! Do you even know how to query? What the hell did you say?"

The Hubs shrugged and glanced at the email on his computer. "Um, basically, 'Hey, I'm Jen, I'm a BFD on social media. I sold a shit-ton of self-pubbed books and now a traditional publisher wants to make me a deal, but I want to shop and see what else is out there. You want in or not?' But more professional than that. Sorta."

Holy hell! "I'm ruined," I sobbed. "That's it. You've ruined me. You've sent out the worst queries in the history of queries. Agents will print it out and share it as what not to do. I'll never get an agent now. Why would you do th—"

Ding! The laptop chimed.

"Look at that," the Hubs said. "Your first reply. Not bad. Ten minutes or so?"

"It's a reply?" I asked. I felt like throwing up. That was

fast. But was it good fast or bad fast? Ugh! "Well, read it already!"

The Hubs scanned the email and got a huge grin on his face. "She's the real deal, Jen. She has legit clients."

"Yeah, yeah," I fumed. "But what did she say? Am I dead to her?"

"No, she wants to call you in the morning."

"Wait. She does?"

"I told you, Jen. I got you."

By the end of the week I had an agent.

How You Can F*cking Do It:

- Find yourself a wing man.
- Turn them loose.
- Seize the day.
- Follow the rules.
- No. Break the rules.
- Scratch that. *Bend* the rules.

12

Let's Write A Book Proposal

"You fail only if you stop writing."

Ray Bradbury

When I signed with my first agent, Mary, we knew we had at least one editor interested in my work, but we wanted to see if we could get other editors interested too.

"The first thing you need is a book proposal," she said.

"Okay," I said. "What's that?"

She explained to me that I couldn't sell a book based on a list of bullet points and a half-assed title, but I also didn't have to write the whole book...yet.

When you're trying to sell a fiction book, you need to have the book finished and in really good shape. I know some authors who hire freelance editors to help them with their manuscript before they ever submit it to agents for consideration. I'm not saying this is a good idea or a bad idea. It really depends upon how much money you have to throw at this process and how much help you want. No matter what, your agent will give you edits before they submit it and then, of course, the editor at the publishing house will give you edits. But if you want to have the best product possible, it might be worth hiring a freelancer to help.

For a nonfiction book you need something called a book proposal. A book proposal is really an outline of the book you're trying to sell—a beefed-up version of the table of contents I'd already submitted to Sarah. It also contains a lot of important information about the author. I was asked to share my social media stats, the number of books I'd sold, and to make a list of who I thought could help me sell this book (this is where it's good to have a crew and strong alliances you can count on). I was asked to compare and contrast myself to others in my genre. "I have the biting humor of Jen Lancaster except I have kids instead of pets and I've never worn pearls in my life. I'm like if Tina Fey was a mommy blogger." In addition to all that, you include a chapter or two that will be in the book. This gives the editor a taste of your voice and what the book might be like.

When Mary told me to write a book proposal, I had no idea what she was talking about, but I did what I always do when I don't have a clue: I turned to Google. (Between Google and YouTube, you can find everything you need to know. What did we do before the internet?) I did a search and found a template I could follow along. It was a very helpful writing site with lots of good information, but it was incredibly dry and boring, so my book proposal ended up incredibly dry and boring.

Mary took one look at the proposal I sent her and she replied with, "What the hell is this?"

"It's my book proposal," I said.

"It's awful," she said.

"Umm...well, I followed the directions... Am I missing a section or..."

"No, it's missing *you*."

"Huh?"

"Are you funny?"

"Yes."

"Is your book going to be funny?"

"Yes."

"Do you have a strong voice?"

"Yes?"

"Yes, you do. Yes, you're funny. But this proposal is tedious."

"I tried to make it professional," I said. "I thought I should tone it down and make it more business-y and shit."

"Yeah, no. That's not right. We need the 'and shit' in there."

"Huh?"

"You are this book. This book is your voice. These are your stories; your proposal needs to reflect that. Make the proposal funny, make it snarky, make it Jen."

"So, can I cuss?"

"Absolutely."

After that conversation I went back to the drawing board and started a new proposal for *People I Want to Punch in the Throat*. I kept the same format that was suggested by the website, but this time I gave it the full Jen Mann effect. I told silly stories, and I included a horribly hilarious picture of myself from middle school complete with a terrible perm and braces. And I made sure I bragged about myself. Not even a humblebrag. I'm talking full-on, "Look at me! I'm the fucking shit!" It was uncomfortable and hard, but I had to do it. ("No one else is going to do it," Mary said. And she was right.)

Writing a book proposal can be kind of exhausting, because it's painful to put yourself out there and to turn all your attention on yourself. It's also hard to know how to package your book. That's where Mary was really helpful. She had the idea to pitch two books in one proposal to publishers.

We had sold thousands of copies of *Spending the Holidays with People I Want to Punch in the Throat*, but it could be improved tremendously. She had the idea to sell the brand-new *People I Want to Punch in the Throat* book along with the self-published edition of *Holidays*. Her idea was the publisher would help me fix *Holidays* and turn it into a better book and then we'd be able to sell it to a wider audience.

I liked her idea, but I thought *Holidays* should be the first book released. It was late summer and my blog always gets a surge of traffic around the holiday season thanks to the still-magical Elf on the Shelf post rising to the top again. My "time of the year" was coming up again, and I thought I could have that book whipped into shape and ready to go for a fall launch to coincide with the wave of new readers that would come. She explained that New York publishing doesn't move near as fast as self-publishing and there would be no way the book would be done in time. She told me we'd need at least a six-month lead to get it out to publications for feature stories. She was also worried that my built-in audience wouldn't want to buy a re-tread. She wanted to lead with the new, unwritten book. "Don't worry about new readers. Your loyal readers have been patiently waiting. They need something new, so we should put *People I Want to Punch in the Throat* out first. You'll retain your fanbase and use that book to grow it. And then the following year we should put out the new and improved *Holidays* edition," she said. "Some of your fans will buy it again, but the new fans you've acquired by then will definitely buy it."

This was sound advice from a sales perspective, so I agreed.

When she took out the book proposal, she was able to get the attention of eight or ten editors. The editors read the proposal and if they like what they see, they usually want to talk to the author before finally making an offer. If you live in the New York City area, it's probably best to do these meetings in person. I've learned that I like to do as many meetings in person as I can, because I don't come across terrific on the phone. I'm not energetic enough, and I can never think of all the questions I want to ask. Plus, I think meeting someone in person is good because you can look them in the eye and really see if you trust what they're saying and you can feel if there's good chemistry. It might seem weird to talk about chemistry, but I truly believe that is what you need for a great publishing relationship. I don't need to the be the godmother of your child, but I do want to make sure we get along easily and are comfortable with one another because we're going to birth a book baby together.

I didn't fly out to New York because I was cheap and I didn't know how important it was to meet in person. So instead, I blocked out an entire day and I set up a marathon of conference calls with my agent and editors.

During each call I took notes and tried to ask the same questions each time so I could compare apples to apples. It was hard, because everyone had a different vision for my books.

"I think these titles would sell well in Spencer's," an editor said.

"Spencer's? Like at the mall?" I asked.

"Yes."

"The place that sold fake vomit when I was in middle school?"

"Yes."

"They're still in business?"

"Yes."

Hard pass.

"I think we could place these books in Anthropologie," another editor said.

"The store where they sell twigs for fifty bucks and every book is about how to decorate your house using books and twigs or cook shit with ingredients you foraged from the woods when you really should have been gathering twigs so you could save yourself fifty bucks?" I asked.

"I take it you're not a fan."

"It's just that I'm just not their people. Like, at all."

I wasn't Spencer's people. I wasn't Anthropologie's people. Whose people was I?

This is a problem a lot of authors run into when they're traditionally published. Traditional publishers are always trying to figure out where they can shelve you. Where can your book live? I wanted my books to live in bookstores, of course. That's why I was doing this! But I also wanted the coveted shelves of Target and Costco.

An editor snorted, "Every author wants her books in Target and Costco. Think outside the box." I wanted to find my people, but I didn't know where they were. I was like, "Do wine stores carry books? Because I think my books would do *ah-may-zing* in wine stores."

No, I was told. Wine stores don't carry books.

Well, I think that's a big mistake. That's a genius idea and you heard it here first.

In the end I chose Ballantine, an imprint of Penguin Random House. I had a few reasons why I went with them:

- Penguin Random House is a BFD in publishing. One of the Big Five. As a child I was that weird kid who actually paid attention to publishing houses, and I remember Random House and Penguin both published a lot of the books I read. They were names I knew and respected.
- The editor brought her entire team on the call. I heard about marketing and publicity ideas. No one else brought the entire team on the call. *I* felt like a BFD.
- They wanted to utilize technology and social media to spread the word about the books and help generate sales. They'd use Pinterest and Instagram and NetGalley to reach potential readers.
- They offered me a lot of money. I'm going to be honest here. We're all motivated by money, right? We all want to get paid for what we do. No matter what it is. An advance is like a salary for a writer. That advance needs to last me the entire length of my contract, because my contract stipulates I can't publish anything else until the contract is up. They didn't offer me the most, but they offered me a lot. I felt like I could accept a little less since I'd have a titan of the publishing industry behind me, but I still asked Mary to negotiate and get some more money. I asked her to at least try and get them to match the higher offer. She got me a solid six figures.

Once you sign the contracts, you get some money. Everyone's contracts are different, so I'll just tell you about mine. My advance was set up in three payments per book, and each book got its own advance and is accounted for separately. When I signed the contract I received one-third of the advance for *People I Want to Punch in the Throat: Competitive Crafters, Drop-Off Despots, and Other Suburban Scourges* and one-third of the advance for *Spending the Holidays with People I Want to Punch in the Throat*. Once I turned in acceptable manuscripts, I received another third. The final third was paid upon publication.

The money was paid to my agent and she took her standard fifteen percent from that amount and then cut me a check for the remainder. I knew when I signed with her that she'd always get fifteen percent of any contract she negotiated for me. Even though our relationship is over, she still continues to get fifteen percent of anything those two books make because she's the one who sold them.

Let me just say something about this fifteen percent. I hear a lot of authors cluck and complain that it's a lot of money to give an agent and I'd like to say, "Are you fucking nuts?" It costs you nothing to sign with an agent, and they only get paid when they get you a sale. Mary earned that fifteen percent by getting me a great deal with a traditional publisher. Mary is the one who built the relationships over the years and the one with the expertise to negotiate the best terms for me. She's the one who helped me write and edit a book proposal SEVEN times before she was satisfied to send it out with her name attached. Mary talked me off ledges and gave me advice that no one else could offer me. Coming from real estate, it always irks me when people say that agents don't "deserve" how much they get paid. As a Realtor, I was one hundred percent commission-based. I had no salary and I only got paid if I sold a house. It might look like all a Realtor does is a drop a sign in your yard, snap some pics, and call it done, but there's a lot going on behind the scenes you don't even know. And that's how I feel about literary agents. They earn every penny. There are many reasons I've chosen to self-publish some of my titles, but "saving" a literary agent's commission isn't one of them.

Okay, rant over.

So, I got the first third and a deadline for *People I Want to Punch in the Throat*'s finished manuscript. I don't remember how long they gave me to write the book, but I do remember I had some say in the matter, so I was comfortable with the timeline. Probably four or five months.

Writing the book is another whole thing. Everyone has their method. I know some writers who send their finished chapters to their agents for feedback. I know some writers who have beta readers who read and give feedback as they write. I know some writers who just write.

I'm the last one. I didn't even know sending stuff to Mary was a possibility. She'd never mentioned it and because I'd never had an agent, I had no idea that was even a thing. It wasn't until I was talking to a friend and she casually mentioned that she texted her agent all day long and emailed her finished pages every night when I was like, "Whaaat? Am I supposed to be doing that?"

I think it's really up to you and how much attention and feedback you want.

I'm a fairly solitary writer. I don't have betas, but my husband usually reads everything I write before I hit publish. I write in spurts and never in a linear way. I start chapters and then abandon them when the creative vein I've tapped runs out. I'm usually working at midnight filling the holes and finishing the chapters. I can't imagine sending such a mess to an agent and hoping for any sort of clear feedback.

When I finished *People I Want to Punch in the Throat* I didn't feel that great about it, actually. It was very different from the proposal I'd pitched and that was because my publishing team had suggested some significant changes that I agreed to. At the time there was another funny lady writer who had an extremely popular book in my genre. Her book was killing it and she was lighting the world on fire. While this book was hysterical, it was also kind of heavy. It dealt with a lot of tough issues and dark periods in this woman's life. We were trying to make my book to be similar, if not the same.

The problem was my tough issues and dark periods weren't really funny; they were just stupid. Also, I hadn't overcome any obstacles even remotely similar to this other writer's struggles. There was no way I could pretend that growing up kind of chubby in an upper middle-class family with two loving parents was such a nightmare. But I tried. Lord, I tried.

I finished the horrible manuscript and sent it off to my editor and Mary, and I waited. And I waited. And I waited. I was worried the publisher would ask for their advance back, and I'd already spent it on a sweet, sweet minivan. I was sure they'd repossess it.

Finally after a month of no news, I got an email from my editor. I don't remember what it said exactly. I'm sure it was an extremely positive and diplomatic email, but in my mind it sounded a lot like, "I read the manuscript. It's shit. I passed it around the office to get twenty-seven other opinions. They agree it's shit. We're very worried about this book and we're not going to make our original publication dates. We have to move them both. You need to write a whole new book, because this one—and I can't stress this enough—is shit. Don't worry, though, we've had a huge, multi-day meeting where we all discussed your shit book, and we've come up with a way forward for you. We think you should write a hilarious book about raising kids in suburbia hell. What do you think?"

What did I think? I think the book I pitched in my original proposal was a hilarious book about raising kids in suburbia hell surrounded by crazy PTA moms and douchey dads and asshole kids. THAT I could do!

It was around this time that I started to worry that my hubris had gotten me into a lot of trouble. *Maybe I've made a mistake*, I thought. I'd been happy self-publishing and I'd done well with it, but my ego wanted to see a book on a shelf. My ego wanted people to stop looking at me with that tinge of judgment.

But that was just me getting in my own way. Did I want to be traditionally published or not? Because being traditionally published meant I had to take other people's opinions into account and I needed to be flexible. My publisher wasn't firing me or repossessing my minivan, they were trying to help me. And deep down I knew my editor was right. Of course that first manuscript was shit. I didn't disagree with that at all. I didn't want that book published any more than she did. The problem was, I knew it would probably be shit when I accepted the changes. I knew it was shit when I turned it in. But I never spoke up. I never argued for what I wanted. And now, because I didn't advocate for myself enough at the beginning of this process, my commitment had stretched from two years to more than three years. And because my contract stated I couldn't publish anything else until the second book came out, just like that, my advance was worth considerably less.

When I tell this story, people ask me if I regret going with a traditional publisher, and my answer is, and always will be, hell no. Yes, it was a learning experience and there were bumps along the way, but they did help me put out two great books that I'm insanely proud of, and thanks to their help, I found a lot of new readers.

There are pros and cons to publishing books, no matter what path you choose, and I don't want to deter anyone from chasing their dream. But I do want to be honest and truthful about my experience so you can avoid the mistakes I made.

How You Can F*cking Do It:

- Listen to the pros.
- Trust your gut.
- Know your strengths and weaknesses.
- Advocate for yourself, no one else will.

13

I Think It Might Be Easier To Find A Spouse Than An Agent

"I love my rejection slips. They show me I try."

Sylvia Plath

Yes, yes, the Hubs broke all the rules when he queried agents, but it worked and I got several replies. But I believe it was only because he specifically mentioned the publisher that was interested in me. Think about it, when I was a Realtor, there was nothing better than getting a phone call from someone who said, "Hi, I need a Realtor, please. I found the house I want, I'm pre-approved to buy it, I have nothing to sell, I am prepared to offer full price, and I can close in thirty days. I just need someone to write the contract. You want in?"

Fuck yeah, I want in! Who wouldn't?

But that's the thing. When you query an agent and you don't have an interested party, it can be a bit more difficult, and it can be met with a bit more resistance. Trust me, I know, because by now I've queried both ways, and the time I had the guaranteed deal was the easiest one. By far.

I don't know if I recommend breaking the rules. Yes, you have to set yourself apart from the herd, but you also have to walk a fine line so you don't appear crazy. I've seen agents sign an author from just the strength of a one-sentence tweet, and I know authors who were signed after a literal elevator pitch at a conference. On the flip side, I've seen agents complain about manuscripts being sent to their homes or writers following them into the bathroom at those same conferences. Read the room, folks. Be aggressive, but don't be a creeper. Follow agents on Twitter and interact when you can. Follow the hashtags and do your research to see that they're a fit. Be ready to reply quickly when an agent responds to your tweet and asks to see your manuscript. Don't put up your pitch and then go on vacation for a week. Oh, and never try to fool them. It's a small, small world, and they talk to one another. Recently I saw an agent out a writer by name. The writer was using the agent's name in her queries to other agents. She said this particular agent had offered her representation but she was shopping around. The agent was like, "Never heard of this bitch," and tons of agents chimed in with, "She's dead to us now."

I say don't break the rules, but like all things related to writing, breaking the rules works sometimes. After the Hubs broke the rules I set up several calls with potential agents so I could find The One.

Here's the thing about agents: they're like boyfriends (or girlfriends). When you're single, you think you want one of those elusive creatures. You see all your friends with their boyfriends and you're like, "Ohh, that would be nice. I'd like to have one of those." But your friends don't tell you that yes, he's a great shoulder to cry on, but also he leaves the toilet seat up after he pees. He's your biggest cheerleader and wants nothing more than to see you succeed, but sometimes he returns phone calls five days after you left a message and he has side chicks. Lots and lots of side chicks. They don't tell you that your boyfriend thinks you're pretty, but at the same time he's also uber picky and he says he knows what he wants in a partner, but when you press him, you realize he really doesn't have a clue. But boyfriends know sexy when they see it, and sexy always gets their attention. So, your friend's best advice is be sexy?

Easier said than done, right? Have no fear, finding an agent isn't that hard or scary, if you're willing to put in the work. You're going to need a spreadsheet and a couple hours a week to really make a dent. Start by compiling a list of agents you want to query. You can find agents through Google searches, referrals from friends, websites, Twitter, conferences, and the acknowledgments section of your favorite book. Their info is out there; you just have to dig it up.

Once you have your list, you need a great query letter. I don't have one. My query letter is a lot of fluff and not a lot of substance. I'm not arrogant enough to think I land agents because of my letter or my writing chops. I land agents because of my sales record and my social media reach. I have proof of concept.

It also might be kind of tempting to sign with the first agent who offers to work with you. For some of you, that might be great. I once heard a very successful children's book author speak at a conference. She talked about starting out and she queried dozens of agents. Only one replied. He was brand new. She would be his first client—his only client. But he connected with her work and he promised to help her (he had nothing better to do). She signed with him and together they went on to create one of world's bestselling children's series and they've been loyal to one another ever since. That's the fairy tale right there. That's what we're all looking for, right?

The first agent who offered to sign me was not like that at all. She was exactly what I imagined a tough New York agent was like...in 1989. She was very gruff on the phone, and maybe it was my vivid imagination, but I could swear I smelled bourbon and cigarettes every time she opened her mouth. She told me she was going to make me "a star." Yeah, she really said that. BUT if I wanted to be a star, I needed to act right now! She knew I had a full day of calls lined up with potential agents, so she was going to fax me a contract (FAX ME) and I'd need to sign it right away and fax it back (FAX IT BACK). As soon as I signed, we'd be an item and I would not even be allowed to speak to those other agents. "Also, there could be some fees involved," she said casually.

This was the first I'd heard of an agent charging fees. "I thought agents take their fees from the deals they make?" I said.

"Yeah, well, I don't work that way. I take a commission then, too, but there are some things we charge for as well. Faxes, long-distance phone calls, postage, maybe marketing. Don't worry about that, though, we'll figure that out as we go along. Now, tell me your fax number."

As much as I wanted an agent, I knew she wasn't the one. I figured I'd rather be single, so I said something like I needed to think about it and hung up the phone. I should not have done that. I didn't need to make an excuse because I was worried about her feelings. She didn't give a fuck about me. I was one of a dozen calls she was going to take that day. This is a huge decision and it can't be made lightly. You don't have an obligation to do anything. You don't owe anyone anything. Yes, it was nice of an agent to take a call with you and spend some time answering your questions, but if you're not vibing with this person, you're completely within your right to say so. Or vice versa.

Later that day I had a call with another potential agent. We talked a bit and then he said, "To be honest, I don't think we're connecting, and I don't think I'd be a good advocate for you. I don't get your sense of humor, but I wish you good luck."

You know what? That was actually great! It might feel like rejection sucks sometimes, but rejection is also good sometimes. Because he was truthful with me, I could strike him off my list and move on. I didn't have to waste time sitting by my phone and hoping he'd call to change his "maybe" into a "yes." He also wasn't a dick about it. He was very frank, but also very polite. He was a professional who didn't try to destroy my ego. He just let me go and I appreciated that, because not everyone was that nice. I had another call, this time with the agent who was the first to respond to Ebeneezer's query. She was a very powerful agent who represented well-known authors and celebrities and I was excited to take her call. She was the kind of agent who could literally change my life. She blew sunshine and rainbows up my ass about what she could do for me. How she loved humor and F-bombs and how I was a great fit for her. She asked me to send her a copy of *Spending the Holidays with People I Want to Punch in the Throat* so she could read it that night and give me her thoughts the next day.

I sent her an e-book and she said, "Thanks, I'll call you tomorrow."

Tomorrow came but no call came. I sent her an email around midday to see if she wanted to get something on the calendar for the next day. No reply. I sent another email. No reply. I called her office. I was told she was

"Currently unavailable but would get back" to me. She never did.

That woman ghosted me. I have no idea what happened. I mean, I'm sure she didn't connect to my material or find me funny, I get that part, but I don't know why she couldn't say that. Because she didn't, I kept making excuses for her. "Maybe she had a family emergency. Maybe one of her clients died. Maybe she had a car accident." Nope. She just didn't want to talk to me again, but she didn't have the common decency to say so. I wasted so much energy fretting over her, but I learned my lesson. Never again. You either like me or you don't. I'm not going to waste time trying to figure out what I did wrong. It's a numbers game. There are hundreds, if not thousands, of agents out there, and I'll keep going.

Interviewing agents can be hard because I'm never sure what I'm supposed to be looking for exactly. I know I want someone who has experience in my genre. For instance, I'm not going to pick someone who represents only science fiction writers and hope she gets me a good deal for my nonfiction humor. But then again, I've talked with agents who are well-respected and connected in my genre and our personalities don't fit together. Or they do fit together, but there's something else holding me back. The agent I liked the most and wanted to be BFFs with only had a couple clients, and at the time I felt like that was a strike against her. Now that I've met with agents who have stables full of writers, I'm not sure I made the right choice. Maybe it would be nice to be the big fish in a small pond?

At this point I've interviewed countless agents and I've signed with three people. All were for different types of personalities, all were for different reasons and at different points in my career.

I signed with my first agent, Mary, because I respected

what she had accomplished with other writers I admired. I liked that she was a mom and she had a sense of humor.

I left Mary because I never felt like I was important to her. I fell in her lap and she was happy to scoop me up and make some money, but she really didn't get what I do, and she was never willing to go out on a limb for me.

At one point, I needed blurbs for my book and my editor told me it was my responsibility to get them. That sort of surprised me, because I was receiving emails and letters through Mary from other authors asking me for blurbs. She'd say, "My friend Anne has a client who would like a blurb" and she'd pass on the note. (FYI, I'm always happy to blurb any book that comes my way. It's a fucking honor and I take it seriously, so I always say yes. And you should too. Think about it—you want to create a tribe, right? Here's a chance to connect with another writer, who already respects you enough to ask for a blurb, so chances are, you could be friends. It's intimidating asking for a blurb; they really put themselves out there and I respect that. Writing a blurb gives you the opportunity to have you name on the cover of yet another book. Book lovers read blurbs and so that gets your name in front of another book lover.)

When it was my turn to get a blurb I asked Mary to send a note to a client of hers I admired. "Ooh, yeah, I don't know," was the response I got. "She's got a lot going on...so..."

"I just need a few words. Not a lot," I begged. "It would make a huge difference."

"I'll see what I can do," Mary said.

A few weeks later my editor was asking again for the blurb, so I followed up with Mary. "Anything yet?" I asked.

"I haven't asked her," Mary said. "She's really overwhelmed right now and I don't want to bother her with..."

With what? With my piddly little book? With my "bold" request?

"Don't worry about it," I said. "I'll get it myself."

And you know what? I did. And you know what else? If she was overwhelmed or bothered by my email, she didn't let me know. She wrote me a blurb, and I know for a fact that blurb sold books for me, because I saw the reviews and comments about her endorsement being the nudge certain readers needed to get the book. Blurbs are very important. Don't take them lightly. And don't take no for answer. I've only ever been turned down once. It wasn't a very polite turn down either. He was kind of an ass, to be honest. I won't name names, but I won't forget. Someday this person (who has already forgotten about his shitty behavior) will come to me for a favor and I'll have to decide then how I'll handle it. I am normally a hotheaded bridge burner, but I'm trying to do better and go with grace and all that shit. Who am I kidding? I'll probably tell him to suck my dick.

When my books finally came out and each sold tens of thousands of copies, none of my team was thrilled. We'd hoped for hundreds of thousands, I guess. I really don't know. Marketing budgets are limited and a lot of times the heavy-hitters get the bulk of the money. I asked for a city bus to be wrapped with my book cover and everyone laughed at me. I wasn't joking. I wanted a bus—maybe even two. I could only sell so many on my own social media platform.

When I talked to Mary about my next book, she sort of shrugged and basically told me I didn't live up to anyone's expectations and I could expect a smaller advance next time.

That was soul-crushing, to be honest.

I get that an agent needs to have tough conversations

with you, but she also needs to understand that you're a fragile artist type and sometimes you need to be handled carefully.

I left Mary and moved on to James. James was the opposite of Mary. He didn't pretend to be anything but the shark he was. I figured if I was going to get my soul crushed, I might as well sign with a known soul-crusher instead of being surprised later on when he revealed his true self to me. James represented a stable of international bestselling authors, and I was microscopic in his world. I was a nobody. I knew going in I was one of his smallest clients, and I had no expectations to be treated the same way he treated his blockbuster clients. I just hoped that with his connections and his drive he'd help propel me to the top of the heap and someday I could be one of his whales who kept his lights on.

Soon after signing with James, I had interest from a legit production company in Hollywood. They wanted to acquire the rights to *People I Wanted to Punch in the Throat* for a television series. I was completely out of my element, so I asked James what we should do. He offered to be on the calls and help me find an LA-based television agent. I think he was on one call maybe. After that he was always too busy to join the calls with me. The production company wanted to move forward, but I needed a television agent. I kept asking him to introduce me and he could never get it done.

The first manuscript I sent James was *My Lame Life: Queen of the Misfits*, my first fiction book for young adults. It was different from my normal genre, but it was a book I really wanted to write. I'd been threatening for years to pivot to fiction, because, honestly, how many more true, funny stories do I have in me? (Answer: at least two more full books.) I wanted to write fiction so I could kill off characters and punch people in the throat for real, but my first attempt was a book inspired by my daughter. At the time she was going through some mean girl shit at school, and I was frustrated. I could see her falling into those same traps so many girls fell into during those awkward tween years. Ladies, can you imagine how badass we would have been in junior high and high school if we had the swagger and confidence we do as forty-year-olds out of fucks to give? I wanted to write a book that would empower Adolpha and girls like her to quit trying to fit their square pegs into round holes. To stop comparing themselves and changing to please others, but instead to accept themselves the way they are. I wanted to write a book to show girls that they need to own their quirks and flaws and to find their tribe and to do it at thirteen and fourteen instead of waiting twenty years like I did.

I channeled two of my muses, Judy Blume and Daria Morgendorffer, and tried to write something that was hilarious and relatable and would speak to a new generation of kids who didn't feel like they fit in. It wasn't too much of a stretch from my adult nonfiction, because I've always written for the person who feels left out and invisible. I also wanted to write a book that showed a normal family life where the drama comes from the most embarrassing people in the world: your loving parents.

It is a book that is impossible to shelve, because there are no dead kids, drugs, dragons, or dystopian nightmares (even though those are my favorite genres to read).

James sat on the manuscript for weeks with little or no feedback. Sometimes he'd check in and say he hadn't had a chance to really put together a good review for me. And then he said he'd lost his copy and could I send it again. That kind of irked me. Whenever he delayed me he'd always blame it on his million-dollar authors and I'd just grit my teeth and think, *It's okay. Someday it will be me he's delaying other people for.* But that's a really shitty thing to think.

Finally he asked for the manuscript one more time and promised to read it that night and be ready for a call in the morning to discuss next steps. I sent it off and waited.

Morning came and he sent me a brief email that basically said he felt the book was "meh" and he did not think he could sell it to anyone and he didn't think it was even worth having a call unless I had something else I was working on.

OOF.

I was *dev-ah-stated*. I felt like I'd wasted so much time and I was on the wrong path and pivoting was wrong and I should have stayed in my lane and if James thought the book was shit, it must be shit.

First he let me down on the television stuff and now this!

I was still spiraling that afternoon when I picked up Adolpha at school. She'd already read the manuscript and she knew I'd been waiting for weeks—nay, months—for a reply from James and that particular day she just happened to ask me, "Hey! Did you ever hear back from your agent about *My Lame Life*?"

I was shocked. "Um, yeah, actually, I heard from him today," I said.

"And? What did he say?"

"Well, he doesn't like it. He thinks it's 'meh' and he can't sell it," I said sadly.

Adolpha snorted derisively. "Well, what does he know? That book is awesome. It's a good thing you know how to self-publish, Mom. And it's a good thing I have a lot of friends who will love it. We'll show him, Mom!"

I fired James the next day and I was ready to make Adolpha my agent.

Instead, I signed with Lori.

Lori came to me recommended by another author friend. We'd been commiserating about the pains of querying and she offered to introduce me to her agent.

I liked Lori a lot. Our phone calls were really fun and upbeat. She loved my pitch and she was anxious to read *My Lame Life: Queen of the Misfits*, and she was excited to take the next steps with me. By that time, I'd taken Adolpha's wise advice and self-published it, and even though it wasn't a mega-hit, it definitely wasn't "meh."

To be honest, I was having a hard time reaching the right audience for it. I'm a huge fan of self-publishing if you can reach your audience. My *People I Want to Punch in the Throat* books do well self-pubbed, because I know where suburban moms aged thirty to fifty-five live on the internet. I know where they shop for books and I know how to speak to them and motivate them to hit that "buy" button. But not all books are good for self-publishing. *My Lame Life* is one of those books.

Teens and tweens are far more elusive. Luring them in is like trying to catch a stray cat. I know they're on Instagram and Snapchat, but I'm, like, trying too hard to be a cool mom, you know? I like to keep it casual and fun and try not scare them off with too many pictures of my minivan and my favorite comfy orthopedic shoes, but it's not working. I do a bit better in person, but I haven't got my pitch down just right for them yet. I have found that if I wear a snarky or sarcastic T-shirt when I do a live event, the kids I'm looking for peel themselves off from the crowd to at least investigate what I'm up to. I still can't make any sudden movements, laugh too loud, or ask anything more personal than, "What do you like to read?"

"I dunno," is the most common retort, and I just nod and say, "Cool, cool, cool."

Do you know who is really good at getting these kids to read?

Traditional publishers.

That's why I signed with Lori. Because I felt like Lori could help me sell *My Lame Life*. I'd sold a self-published book to a publisher before and I was confident I could do it again. I felt like *My Lame Life* was actually the perfect book for this, because when James looked at it, he immediately thought it was hard to shelve, thus hard to sell to a traditional publisher. There's no romance, there's no real drama, there's no magic or end-of-the-world stuff; it's just an average girl trying to get through her life with sarcasm and heart.

By self-publishing that book and selling thousands of copies of it and getting really awesome reviews on it, I'd proven there was a market for it and maybe it wasn't such a risky chance for a publisher.

Lori agreed with me. But she suggested "a few" edits before we sent it out. We definitely had different ideas of what "a few" meant. It was basically a rewrite.

After rewriting *People I Want to Punch in the Throat*, I was reluctant to do much. But I was also ready to hear it all, because the book wasn't as successful as I wanted and I needed help. So I took all the notes Lori and her team gave me and I made all the changes, and really, I was quite happy with the final product. It wasn't exactly what I had in mind, but it was good, and if Lori thought she could sell it, then I was happy with the results.

I sent it off and waited.

But then I went into the Cone of Silence again. Lori and her team went dark and every time I asked for an update or feedback, I was ignored. If I did get an answer it was weeks later and a brush-off.

I couldn't believe it. Again? Ugh.

Maybe it's me? I wondered. *Maybe I'm a terrible writer? Maybe I'm difficult? Maybe I want too much?*

I don't know, I have over a million fans on social media and I've sold hundreds of thousands of books. I don't think a terrible writer can accomplish that. Difficult? I like to think I have high standards for myself and the people who surround me. If that's difficult, then I don't want to be easy. I definitely want a lot, but not too much. I realize no one is going to be as invested in my career as I am, but I don't think it's too much to ask for timely responses and helpful criticisms and a cheerleader in my corner.

So, I did it again. I parted ways with yet another agent and decided to go it alone.

I drifted for a few months after that, trying to decide what to do with my life. Around the same time I was having trouble with my eyes. I was struggling to find an answer as to why my vision was so blurry and my eyes wouldn't stop itching and burning. I couldn't read. I couldn't write. I couldn't see anything except a fog over everything. *Maybe it's a sign,* I thought. I'm not big on signs, but when you're going blind, it's kind of sign, right?

Was I really going to give up writing? But what would I do for a living? Go back to real estate? I could do that, sure. But would I be happy? Absolutely not.

I'll be honest, I wallowed a bit. I was angry (but not my usual "get shit done" angry) and I felt like all the good mojo I'd had before was used up. My luck had run out, and now what was I going to do? I was going to fail. I was going to be a quitter. Yeah, I could blame it on my eyes, but I would know the truth. It was just me feeling sorry for myself. I could buy more technology and hire more people to help me keep going. I just didn't want to do the work. I was exhausted. I felt like every time I had something figured out and it was working for me, the goal line moved.

That's the thing about this business. Yeah, you're the captain of your own ship, but sometimes you have no idea where the fuck you're going, because everything keeps changing. You have to be agile and flexible. You have to be proactive as well as reactive. You have to be aggressive, but also cautious. It can be a mindfuck, and I was letting it get to me. I knew it wasn't my eyes holding me back. It was me again and my old friend: fear.

Fucking fear, man.

Fear of failure is the thing that keeps me up at night.

One night I couldn't sleep. I couldn't stop thinking about terrible perms I'd had in middle school and that one time in 1995 I told a 7-Eleven employee "Love you" instead of "Thank you." After a while, we got to my current shitty career situation. *What are you even doing with your life?* I asked myself. *Should you stop writing? Should you keep writing? Should you continue querying and hope to find your soul mate?*

There was a great deal of tossing and turning and doing some serious soul-searching and real-talk with myself. But this time instead of being scared, I got angry, and this time it was my "get shit done" kind of angry. I devised a plan (at least it's my plan for now, but the good thing about plans is they can always change):

- I would keep writing, and I'd write what I wanted to write. I know me. I know what I do best. I need to stay in my land and own that motherfucking lane.
- I could keep writing because I'd found a team of doctors who were fixing my eyes and I was feeling better every day. I'd follow my strict treatment regimen and I *would* recover.
- I'm a kick-ass self-publisher. If I write what I

want to write, I know I can sell it. It might take longer on my own, but I have nothing but time and energy, and I'd rather put that effort into myself. Plus, I'll keep control, and I have the potential to make more money during the long-term.
- BUT because I want to keep a foot in each world, I will also query agents. Not every book is meant for self-publishing and I'll need an agent again someday.
- No more worrying about everyone else's shit. Time to put on my blinders and get to work. I'd been going down the shame spiral of comparing myself to others, and nothing good comes from that. Lifting others up is always good, but comparison is soul-sucking and time-consuming.
- If I have time to lay, I have time to slay, or some witty badass shit like that. I got out of bed that night and started writing again.

How You Can F*cking Do It:

- Do your research.
- Don't fear rejection.
- Keep trying.
- Don't be afraid to break up.
- Consider all your options.
- Make a plan.
- But keep it flexible.

14

Let's Make Some Money

"Writing is one of the few professions in which you can psychoanalyze yourself, get rid of hostilities and frustrations in public, and get paid for it."

Octavia E. Butler

Every writer loves to write, but we also like to pay our bills, so the ultimate goal is to make some dollar bills, right?

People ask me if you can make a living writing and my answer is always yes, BUT there isn't one path to money, though. You need to have several revenue streams going at once. I know lots of writers, but I don't know any who are living off only writing one book every few years. I think those days are over for a lot of people. Everyone I know is diversified and many still have full-time jobs and write on the side.

I've been writing full-time for a few years now and I

have many, many, many revenue streams. It can be a lot to keep up with, but to me it beats having an office job. I never want to go back to a cubicle again, so I will figure out ways to earn an income through my writing (preferably without wearing a bra or real pants).

Here's where I make money:

Advances and royalties from traditional publishers. I got an advance when I signed my traditional-publishing contract. Usually it is broken into segments. For instance, I got one-third upon signing, one-third upon turning in an acceptable manuscript, and one-third upon publication.

An advance is kind of like a loan and you have to "earn out" before you get any royalties. I'm asked a lot how many books you need to sell before you earn out. This is complicated math determined by the publisher. They track your sales and the price the book or e-book sold for and they allot you a dollar (or coin) amount toward your advance. So, a hardcover book retailing for full price is worth more than an e-book on sale for ninety-nine cents. Once their convoluted math tells them they've recouped their investment, you earn a royalty. The royalty is a percentage of each sale going forward. Every six months you receive a statement from the publisher showing you the breakdown of units sold, money allotted toward your advance, and what you still owe. Today I received my latest royalty statement, and after five years I am now three hundred dollars away from "earning out." By this time next year I'll be receiving royalty checks. They won't be much, because my percentage is not that high and Mary, my former agent, will take her fifteen percent as well. I don't know if that was fast or slow, but I know that I've met a lot of authors who have never earned out, so I feel like it's an accomplishment if nothing else. I want to the publisher to feel like I was a good investment and if I earned them back all their money, then I'd say I was. The good news about an advance is if you don't earn out, you don't have to pay back the publisher.

Royalties from self-publishing. As I write this, I have fourteen self-published titles available for purchase at different price points. Some are available in e-book only, and some are available in e-book and physical book form. Because I'm self-published across multiple platforms (KDP, B&N, iBooks, Kobo, etc.) I get royalties from each of the sites selling my books. They don't give me an advance. Instead, they host my books for free on their sites and they give me a share of the revenue every time a book is sold.

Audio rights, international rights, television/movie rights. I've sold the audio rights and international rights for several of my books now. I've been offered television rights, but it hasn't been the right project for me yet. I've retained a manager this year, and I'm hoping that with his help we'll be able to put together something awesome.

Freelancing. I personally don't do much freelancing, but I know a lot of writers who do it as either a supplemental income or as a full-time job. There are freelancing opportunities out there, but you have to be ready to HUSTLE.

My friend Kim Bongiorno is a very successful freelancer and we shared a hotel room together a few years ago at a conference. I woke up the first morning to find Kim already on her laptop sending out emails. I was hungry and wanted to go downstairs to get the free breakfast and Kim said, "Hang on a sec, I'm almost done here and then I can go with you."

"What are you doing?" I asked.

"Sending out my pitches for today." And then she showed me she'd pitched five ideas to ten publications. I'm not very good at math, but I think that's fifty ideas. In. One. Day. Kim knew they wouldn't all be accepted, but she hoped at least five or six of them would be. And she knew that even if her ideas weren't accepted today, she'd have new ones for her editors tomorrow. I have a hard time coming up with enough ideas to fill a couple of books and blog posts every year; I can't imagine coming up with fifty ideas a day! But that's the kind of dedication and perseverance it takes. Kim's a machine and a professional and nothing gets in the way of her pitches. That's how you become a successful freelancer.

Ad revenue from the blog. When I first started blogging I ran lots of ads on my site. It was ugly and annoying for readers, but it was the only way I could afford to blog five days a week. It used to be quite lucrative for me, but over the years, the ad companies changed their payout structures. Over time it became less and less profitable. I was also getting flagged a lot for "indecent content" because I swear like a motherfucker and talk about vaginas and shit. I was being policed all the time and it was driving me crazy. After a while, I took down all the ads because the trouble wasn't worth the money I was making.

Affiliate ads. I took down the ads on my blog except for affiliate ads. I leave those up because they are not as intrusive, not as puritanical, and they're helpful. I'm always recommending books, leggings, bras, hair products, you name it, and it's nice to have an affiliate ad I can throw up there and make a few dollars on. These are especially good during the holiday months. I already have increased blog traffic during that time of year and people are out shopping, so I make the most off affiliate ads then.

Sponsors. This is like affiliate ad revenue but different. Affiliate ads are me specifically creating a unique, trackable link and sharing it with my endorsement. I only make money when someone buys that product. When you sign up for ads on a blog, the companies you sign up with are the ones who go out and find the advertisers and serve them up to your readers. The ads are specific to the reader. So when some woman sends me an email complaining about the smutty ads she's seeing on her desktop, I'm like, "Do you have a teenage son?" Because the ad companies know what is being searched for on that computer and they're choosing ads based on the search history of that device. We all have this sneaking suspicion that Facebook and Google and Amazon are listening to us—well, I'm here to tell you it's for real. They're snooping in your emails and messages and watching your search history and that's why you're seeing the ads you see.

Sponsors are different, though. Sponsors are particular companies that I contract with and agree to write about on my blog. There are lots of bloggers out there who do a brisk business with sponsorships.

I think it's incredibly hard to be authentic and be good at writing sponsored material. It's a true gift, and I don't have that gift. There is no way in the world I could go on about the benefits of life insurance or why I choose mop A over mop B when I wax my floors, but if you can do that well, you can make good money. I know really talented bloggers, YouTubers, and Instagrammers who make six figures a year through partnerships. Many of them have a full-time assistant who does nothing but go after these lucrative deals.

Another reason why I don't do much sponsored work is because I've never had a "family-friendly" blog, so brands are leery to work with me. It's too bad, because I have done some brand work in the past and when it's a good fit for me and my voice, it can work really well. I've worked with Honda and Shoebox. I've had an ongoing relationship with Responsibility.org for years that has been a great experience for my audience and me. It actually makes me sad more brands don't take a chance on me, because I can sell the shit out of leggings, bras, and hair products.

Consulting. Brands are leery to have me write anything for them, but they're not afraid to pay me to pick my brain. I've been contacted over the years by several companies who pay me to tell them "what moms want" or help them market better to middle-age women. I've been hired by some of the top advertising agencies in the world to help advise their clients.

These kinds of gigs are a bit tougher to get. If this is what you want, I'm not even sure how to tell you to get started. It sort of fell into my lap when the first ad agency reached out to me. After that, I think word got around that I'm full of great ideas and I'm a blast at board meetings or something like that, because I got more offers to work together.

Brands may not want me to put my official stamp of approval on their product, but they definitely value my input, and I don't care how we work together as long as they pay me.

Coaching. My inbox is full of requests from writers who are looking for advice. I would love to be able to answer them all, but if I did that, I'd never get my own work done. So I started consulting with them. I only take on a few clients every year and I coach them over Skype. I'm not cheap, but I'll hold your hand and help you get shit down. You can always email me for my rates and availability.

Speaking. When I first started writing I was anonymous and planned to stay that way forever. I already got enough negative comments about my opinions; I didn't want to hear how bad my hair looked too. So, the idea of getting up in front of a group of people and speaking sounded like a nightmare to me.

But after attending a couple of writing and blogging conferences I got irritated because so much of what the speakers were sharing was completely unhelpful and I barely considered them to be a success. I remember sitting in the audience thinking, "Really? This is the best you could find? I know more than she does."
I probably ran my mouth at one of the organizers and she probably said, "Okay, then let's see you do better," or something like that. But I couldn't because I didn't have any experience. I needed to gain some speaking skills, and I needed to practice before I got up on a stage and tried to do it in front of a conference room full of paying people.

So I started at libraries, because libraries are always

looking for content and they never charge people to attend. Basically it was a free, captive audience for me to try stuff out on.

I remember one of the first things I did was teach a class about social media for small businesses. I had this whole PowerPoint presentation thing ready to go and I was going to UNLOAD a fuck-ton of wisdom on these people. I got about two minutes in when a man in the back raised his hand.

"I have a question," he said.

"Yes?" I said.

"This is all very interesting, but what is social media?" he asked.

I was very confused. "Well, it's, uh, it's why you're here."

"Yes, but, like, what is it?" he asked again.

Half the room nodded.

"And where is it?" a woman in the front asked.

The other half of the room nodded.

"So, you guys have, like, no ideas what social media is or even where to find it?" I asked.

They shook their heads.

Oh, fuck me, I thought. My whole presentation went out the window because I had to start at the very beginning of time. "Once upon a time, Alexander Graham Bell invented the telephone..." and go from there.

I got out of there and immediately pitched a new session called "What Is Social Media and Where to Find It." It was standing room only.

Libraries are looking for content, but your content can't be, "Hi, I'm a writer and I want to tell you why you should buy my book." That's not going to fly. They typically want you to teach their attendees something. Especially if you're just getting started. In the beginning I spoke at the library for free and really honed my skills and my presentations. I figured out what worked and what didn't work. I learned a lot, and then I was ready to get paid.

Now I have about ten topics I can speak or teach about. I speak at conferences, libraries, schools, corporate events, and more. I've been on panels and led round tables and I've been a keynote speaker. I'm also at the point now where libraries contact me and pay me to come in and promote whatever new book I have. I have a reputation as a funny and entertaining speaker, and I get a lot of those opportunities through librarians talking to one another and recommending me.

I also host my own reader events around the country. I started doing that when I published *Working with People I Want to Punch in the Throat: Cantankerous Clients, Micromanaging Minions, and Other Supercilious Scourges*. It had been a few years since I'd gone on the road, and my readers were asking me if I was going on tour. I told them touring kind of sucks. I love getting out there and meeting my readers and entertaining them, but I hate sitting in a bookstore hoping people will show up. People always say they're going to come, but then life or anxiety or traffic happens, and I'm sitting there by myself. Also, it's kind of expensive to go on the road. No. Not kind of expensive. It is expensive. And I didn't have a publisher behind me this time. I'd self-published *Working*, and I was on my own for this tour.

I made a joke that I'd rather visit someone's town and hang out in a bar with twenty-five of their closest friends than sit in a bookstore by myself. The response was overwhelming.

"I'll do that!"

"Come to my house and stay in my guest room!"

"I can make that happen this week!"

At first I thought it was a joke, but the more I talked to them, I realized these people were dead serious. All right, then. Now I needed to make it worth putting on pants and leaving my house. I asked for hosts and hostesses to help me. What I said was, "I don't know your town as well as you do, so I need you to find me a space, and I need you to help me get people in the door." I came up with the idea to pre-sell "tickets" to the event. The ticket would get attendees a copy of *Working with People I Want to Punch in the Throat* and an evening of entertainment. If, for some reason, they couldn't make it, I'd mail them the book.

I needed a minimum of twenty-five attendees before I'd get on a plane.

At this point, I think I've hit about fifty stops on this "tour," and I'm heading back out on the road soon. It's been so much fun to connect with people in such an easy and relaxed manner. My hosts and hostesses have been amazing, and I could not have done it without them.

A question I'm asked a lot is, "Does it make money?"

And the answer is yes and no.

To me, I look at a book tour as a publicity stunt. It's not about selling books; it's about spreading the word. It's about meeting people and making them super fans. I did make money because I brought other titles with me that I could sell in addition. I'd see an uptick in online sales when people would talk about seeing me live and the FOMO would kick in. I had hundreds of people sharing photos of my books and tagging me on social media, which is great exposure. So yes, I made money. Not every stop was a moneymaker, but other stops made up for the previous one's loss. Overall, the tour made money. But not a lot. Not enough for me to say, "Yes, go do this and make a mint."

All this to say, don't be afraid to try new things, to take a risk, because who knows? It might be worth it.

How You Can F*cking Do It:

- Have multiple revenue streams.
- Take risks, try new things.
- Know your worth and ask for more.
- Get paid, but don't sell out.

15

Publish An Anthology

"Alone we can do so little; together we can do so much."

Helen Keller

After the success of self-publishing *Spending the Holidays with People I Want to Punch in the Throat*, I was inundated with pleas for help from other writers. To many, it seemed like I'd come out of nowhere and stumbled upon some kind of secret to success.

"How did you do it?"

"How did you go viral?"

"How did you get a self-published book to hit the top of the Amazon charts?"

"How, how, how?!"

I didn't have any answers for them, because at that point I wasn't even sure how I did it. I knew that I'd had some luck when the Elf on the Shelf blog post went viral, and I knew I'd put in a lot of hard work to keep that "luck" going. I'd worked tirelessly to capitalize on that one hit. Through trial and error I'd figured out how to write and self-publish a book. I knew that I'd made a ton of mistakes, but I'd also learned a lot.

I really wanted to help them, but I didn't know what to do exactly.

In those days I'd been following a group of super successful indie authors online. They were romance and thriller writers, but just because we wrote different genres didn't mean I couldn't learn something from them. I find that no matter what someone writes, if I listen carefully, I'll learn something. They were kind enough to let me lurk in the shadows and learn from their example. I'd noticed that they worked together a lot of times. They'd formed a tribe and they'd cross-promote one another's new releases and they'd trade newsletter ads. They were always dropping pearls of wisdom, and sometimes I listened and sometimes I thought I knew better. Looking back now, I realize I didn't know better and I should have listened closer.

For instance, I was invited to a private party they hosted and I found myself talking to one of the most accomplished authors in the bunch. The self-published version of *Spending the Holidays with People I Want to Punch in the Throat* was out and I was selling what I thought was a decent number of books, but when she dropped her sales numbers on me, my jaw practically hit the floor.

"Holy shit. How are you able to get so many sales?" I asked.

"I have a newsletter," she said. "Do you have a newsletter?"

I shook my head. "No, I have a Facebook page. It has 180,000 followers," I said proudly.

She grimaced. "Yeah, but Facebook controls those

people, not you. If you had them all in a newsletter, you could reach them on your own terms."

Always the cheap one, the Hubs said, "180,000 subscribers to a newsletter can be pricey."

She shrugged. "Maybe. But imagine how many books you'd sell. You'd more than pay for it."

"How many subscribers do you have?" I asked.

"Twenty-five thousand," she replied.

I picked my jaw off the floor so I could drop it again. "Wait. You're selling that many books with only 25,000 subscribers?"

"Yep."

"Wow."

"You should really start a newsletter," she said.

"Yeah, I'll think about it. Thanks," I said.

The Hubs and I drifted away, and to be honest, we weren't sure we believed her. We didn't know her that well, and we didn't know anyone putting up the kinds of numbers she was talking about. It seemed damn near impossible to us. (I'd like to say that she was one hundred percent truthful and over the years she actually beat those numbers and snagged a seven-figure contract from a major publisher. I was a fucking moron.)

I didn't do what she suggested. I convinced myself that romance readers were different from humor readers. Stupid, stupid, stupid. I convinced myself the expense of a newsletter wasn't worth it. So dumb. I had 180,000 followers on Facebook in those days and I was positive they'd all sign up for my newsletter and cost me thousands of dollars. Moron!

The only thing I was right about was there was no way in hell I could produce as many titles as she did. She was releasing a full-length book every six weeks. My head spun just thinking about that. "Humor is harder to whip up than romance," I lied to myself.

I should have gone straight home that night and started a newsletter list (and at least one more book), but I didn't. Another one of my big mistakes.

That night wasn't a complete loss, though. I did listen to one idea they had, and it's worked out really well for me.

These ladies were all successful, but not all of them had hit the bestseller lists, which is something an author desires deep down in her heart. At the end of the day we like to write books and sell books and all that jazz, but what we really want is to see "bestselling author" next to our names. So they came up with a plan. They all contributed one book to an anthology and then they worked their tails off together. With their combined social media reach and newsletter juice and sales skills, they got that book onto every list that counts. After that, every single one of those ladies could join the ranks. They'd all earned a spot.

I decided an anthology could accomplish a few things for me:

1. I could release another book like I was advised to do, but I was too tired to write. If we all worked together, it would lift the burden and would be easier. I knew how to self-publish now, and I was positive I could sell it to my audience for sure. I was positive if we worked together we'd definitely be able to get that book to the top of the charts.
2. I could create some luck and opportunity for all the people who had reached out to me. By then I had several editors and websites following me, and I knew they'd read the book. And maybe if

they found something they liked, they'd offer some paying gigs.
3. Maybe I'd hit a list? At that point I hadn't hit any list except "Amazon bestseller," and I could taste "*New York Times* bestseller."

I started planning my anthology. I bought the romance anthology as research. (I buy a lot of books as research.) I figured out right away that the formula was going to need some adjustment for my contributors and me. The romance writers all chipped in an entire book for their anthology. (I'd really call that a box set, but whatever.) I knew we couldn't each write a whole book, but we could write one story. If I put thirty-five to forty together, that would make a whole book. But what would we write? I decided to look at what was popular with my audience. I went through my blog archives to see which posts had been read and shared the most. A theme emerged: hilarious motherhood stories—the more awkward, cringy, heartwarming, and/or relatable, the better.

Because I'd never done anything like this, I was a bit nervous. I wanted to try it, but I wanted it to be a safe space for me. I decided not to announce an open call for submissions. I was still keeping a very low profile in those days, and I knew I'd have to interact with my contributors, so I wanted them to be people I trusted. I knew I really didn't want any dudes. No offense, fellas. I love you guys a lot, but I'm all about the girl power. If you want to go viral, go live and load the dishwasher. Plus, this book was going to be about motherhood. The last thing anyone wanted to read was a some guy's take on motherhood. Hard pass. I made a list of forty female writers I either knew personally (hello, girl gang) or admired from afar. And one invitee was plucked from my comments section. I loved Rachael's witty comebacks on my blog posts, and I wanted to see what she could do with a full-length essay. Once I had my list, I sent out an email and explained what I wanted to do. Thirty-five came back with, "You had me at hello" or something like that. I set a deadline and everyone got to work.

Because I was the publisher I had to do all things again, only I did them right this time.

I had my theme, but I needed a title. For me, titles are the worst. I'm terrible at titling blog posts or articles, and up until that point I'd only titled one book, so I didn't know much about titles. I knew that it needed to be funny and slightly irreverent, because that's my thing. I like my titles to make people laugh or stop walking. I want readers to know instantly if it's a book for them or not.

I'd seen enough people do a double take at *Spending the Holidays with People I Want to Punch in the Throat* that I knew I'd need something as catchy. I started by thinking about me:

- Middle-age.
- Suburban.
- Biological mother of two.
- Married.
- Married to a man.

I needed something every mother could relate to. I couldn't catch everyone in my net, but I could at least adjust my mindset so I could include as many as possible.

- Not all moms are middle-age, and I'd eliminate entire age groups if I went with middle-age in the title.
- Not all moms are suburban. I knew I had a lot of readers who were city and country folk.

- Not all moms have two kids; some have singletons, some have twenty, and a lot have everything in between.
- Not all moms birthed their babies.
- Some moms are on their own.
- Some moms are married to other moms.

I made a list of words that described "motherhood" to many of the people on that list and because I'm a complainer my list immediately went to the pain points of motherhood: messy, late, frumpy, harried, frazzled.

And then it came to me.

What does every mother, no matter how many children she has, no matter what her partner is like, dream of?

Peeing alone.

I Just Want to Pee Alone was born.

Ben came up with another amazeballs cover for me and when it was time to publish the book, the thirty-six of us worked together to push that book as high up the charts as we could.

I put together a plan of attack. We all had different skills, and it was helpful to work together. Somebody wrote a press release, another person made promotional graphics, and another worked on a script for a video. It was nice to have so many women working together to achieve the same goal.

With our combined reach and contacts, we got a lot of press coverage for the book. There was a lot of competition in the "mommy book" category, but we managed to break out from the pack and set ourselves apart.

I Just Want to Pee Alone didn't shoot right to the top. Instead, it was a grower, not a shower. It has continued to sell thousands of copies every year. It is also my only self-published book that hit the *New York Times* bestseller list. It didn't hit the first week it was published. It didn't even hit the first year it was published. When that book was two years old, I got a Google Alert that something had been printed about the book. I was surprised, because a two-year-old book rarely gets press. I clicked the link and found what had triggered the alert: a spot on the *New York Times* bestseller list.

I'd gone to an author panel a few months before I decided to publish *I Just Want to Pee Alone*. It was an all-female panel of YA fiction writers. One of the panelists had just had a massive breakout hit and the moderator asked the others, "Are you jealous of her success?"

What a fucked-up question to ask!

Everyone was silent for a minute, unsure what to say, and then the wisest one at the table spoke up and said something like, "Absolutely not. We are all YA authors, and she is breaking ground and paving the way for us to come behind her. We are thrilled for her success, because success for her is success for us. Her readers are now buying our books. She's shown retailers our genre needs more shelf space. When the water rises, all boats rise."

She was butchering John F. Kennedy's famous quote, "A rising tide lifts all boats," but I got what she was saying. Her speech has stuck with me since then. Her quote is a mantra I live by, and it's what I keep as my North Star when I was publishing *I Just Want to Pee Alone*.

After witnessing the power of our collaboration and the opportunities it presented, I knew I had to continue publishing anthologies every single year, and I'm proud to say I haven't missed one yet.

These anthologies give me a sense of purpose, and they provide me with a way to give back to my community. I found success, and I don't want to pull up that ladder behind me. I want to leave it there and help others climb it too.

I added it up the other day and I have more than one-hundred-and-sixty contributors published in my anthologies. Out of those one-hundred-and-sixty contributors, I've had many go on to have successful creative careers.

Some have gone on to be *New York Times* bestselling authors in their own right, some have profitable writing careers, many earn an income from freelancing, and a few do incredibly lucrative work with brands. One even has an Emmy award for her writing on *Last Week Tonight with John Oliver*.

When I first started publishing the *Pee Alone* books, I thought I was doing it for the audience, but over the years I've come to realize, I was doing it for the community these books created.

I haven't had the pleasure of meeting all one-hundred-and-sixty contributors, but when I do, it's like a family reunion. In fact, I call us the "Pee Family" whenever I'm talking about the group as a whole. I feel incredibly lucky to know each one of them and to know their words touched me enough that I had to include them in my books. They're all special to me, and I am always available to help any of them in any way I can. I don't feel like a mother, exactly, but I do feel a real bond with them. A few years ago, Beth, one of my contributors passed away, and even though I'd never met her in person, it was a very painful loss. She knew she was dying when she wrote an essay for *I STILL Just Want to Pee Alone*, and it is still one of the most heart-wrenching things I've ever read, and I miss her and her fierce, funny, honest, raw, thought-provoking words dearly. This is what creating a community can do for you. It can bring people into your lives, even for a brief time, who touch you and make an impact on you and your outlook on the world.

How You Can F*cking Do It:

- Other writers aren't your competition, they're your allies.
- Collaborate, collaborate, collaborate.
- There's strength in numbers.

16

Put On Some Pants And Leave The House

> **"Do one thing every day that scares you."**
> Eleanor Roosevelt

In the fall of 2017 I published *Working with People I Want to Punch in the Throat: Cantankerous Clients, Micromanaging Minions, and Other Supercilious Scourges.* I self-published that one, because Random House passed on it. I had a clause in my contract that allowed Random House to have the first look, but my editor was under-whelmed. She didn't see the potential, so she passed.

At first I was kind of irritated, because what kind of logic is that? I'd sold tens of thousands of copies of my other books by then and I wasn't a risk by any stretch of the imagination. But this is where it can be tricky to work with big publishers. They have a plan and if you don't fit into their plan, there isn't room for you. They'd had a hard time classifying my first two books. Were they humor? Were they memoir? Were they parenting? I wasn't a celebrity, so why would anyone care about my pedestrian life in the Midwest? At the end of the day, the publishers want a guaranteed hit and I wasn't a guarantee. It wasn't personal, it was business.

However, when my editor passed, my agent decided it wasn't worth taking the proposal out to other publishing houses, because if Random House didn't want me, why would anyone else?

Ugh, fucking fucked up logic. That was fine with me, because I was ready to move on. I'd been tied into a contract for three years and couldn't publish anything related to People I Want to Punch in the Throat during that time. I was anxious to get something new out there and try to recapture the momentum I'd lost being tied down for three years. I didn't care what the publisher or my agent said, I knew I could market *Working with People I Want to Punch in the Throat* and sell it on my own.

I hired an editor and I paid Ben to create a kick ass cover. It felt good to be in charge of my own destiny again.

When the book came out, it was a decent seller, but I needed something to really goose the sales and I wasn't sure what to do exactly.

At the same time my readers were asking me if I was going to on a book tour to promote the new book. I hadn't been on a tour for three years and to be honest, it hadn't been a really good experience for me. It was a lot of me sitting in empty bookstores and hoping people would show up. It was me traveling to major cities and having people complain that I was on the "wrong side" of town. Motherfuckers, I'm in Atlanta metro. Pack some snacks and get in your car and get your ass over here, because this is a lot closer than Kansas City! And when you're a self-published author, bookstores aren't that supportive, because they see self-publishing as their enemy. I'm not their enemy. I'm just an author trying to sell some books and I can't help it that your competition is the one who prints them for me. I knew it would be hard to get bookstores to host me and I wasn't sure what else I could do, so I kind of ignored the requests.

However, one day, when someone posed the question to me yet again on Facebook I made a flippant remark. Something like, "I hate going on tour. I'd rather come to your city and go to your favorite bar and meet you and twenty-five of your best friends and entertain you guys and sell you books."

I walked away from the computer for a bit and when I returned I had dozens of messages:

"Yes! Let's do it!"

"I own a bar, come here."

"How far are you willing to travel?"

"Are you serious because I have thirty people right now who would come to my living room and see you."

It fed my ego, but that was about it. I didn't reply to anyone. However later that night I mentioned the exchange to Ebeneezer. "Isn't that a silly idea?" I said. "Me traveling around and meeting people in bars and stuff."

"Hang on," he said, pondering. "Let's think about this. Bookstores are tough because you're self-pubbed, but also people were reluctant to show up when you weren't right in their neighborhood or whatever."

"Yes."

"But if you literally hang out in their living room, they'll show up, right?"

We started brainstorming and we can up with a plan. I

contacted my readers who had expressed interest in having me visit and I asked them to help me.

I explained that I didn't know their city very well and I needed them to help me find a venue. Preferably a free venue. I suggested bars or restaurants with private rooms. We'd pick a slow night, a Tuesday or Wednesday, and we'd promise to bring in at least twenty-five people who wanted to drink and eat. If that didn't work, then I suggested my hostess team up with a library. Like I said before, libraries are a great resource and if you give them enough notice, they will usually work with you. Even if they didn't want to host, they might have a community room that can be reserved for a private party.

Once we had a venue locked down, then I asked my hostess to gather up her friends and pre-sell tickets. I would help promote the event too, but when I'm going to some place like Syracuse, New York, I'm not a lot of help. I don't have a huge following in Syracuse. (Or do I? Let me know if you're out there, Syracuse!) I explained that I couldn't leave my house unless we pre-sold at least twenty-five tickets.

The "tickets" get each attendee a book. Sometimes we will add a bit more to the ticket price if we needed to cover the cost of a room rental or if we decided to serve appetizers or give one drink or something like that. It just depended upon the hostess and the venue. I think the most expensive ticket we had was about thirty dollars.

I used PayPal, Square, and Fyllan to accept payment in advance and then when the time came, I'd pack my bags and head off to Syracuse, New York or Madison, New Jersey. I didn't have to guess how many books to bring, because I'd already pre-sold them. I always brought more copies, though, because I knew that people would buy other titles for themselves or to give as gifts.

At my first stop I realized I had no idea what I was doing. I had sort of envisioned me holding up a wall in a room full people while they all socialized with one another and then someone would announce books were available, I'd sign them, and head back to my hotel to take off my pants and watch Netflix. What I realized was that was boring as hell and my party was quickly becoming a dud.

"You should say something," my hostess whispered in my ear as she surveyed the restless crowd.

"Like what?" I whispered back, panicked.

"I don't know. What do you usually say?"

I thought about it. On my last tour the bookseller would thank everyone for coming and read my bio and then I'd read a chapter from my book, take a couple questions, and that would be it. It really wasn't a great formula, because it was a lot of reading and not a lot of interacting with my guests.

Earlier that summer I'd been contacted by a small library. They'd sent me an email asking me to "Do the People I Want to Punch in the Throat show." I had no idea what they meant by that, but I couldn't let on. What are those rules? Fake it until you make it and always say Yes, and... all that good stuff, right?

So, I replied with a friendly email saying that I'd love to come and do the 'show' but could they remind me what show they had in mind, please? I made it sound like I have so many shows and I couldn't possibly keep track of them all.

The librarian responded with, "You know, your origin story or whatever."

My origin story, I thought. *Right. That one.*

Spoiler alert: I still had no idea what she was talking about, but I couldn't keep asking for details, I had to just create my origin story and go with it.

And that's what I did. I drove a couple of hours to a small bar in Kansas and I got a little liquid courage in me and I spun a tale. I told them my origin story and much to my surprise, it killed. Everyone laughed and had a great time and I sold a bunch of books.

So, several months later when I was sitting in that dying room trying to figure out how to breathe lift back into it, I knew what I had to do.

"I need a mic," I told my hostess. "I know what I'm going to say."

After that, I worked on my story at every stop. I watched the crowd's responses and I figured out what was the funniest way to say something. I trimmed the fat and whittled down the time so it didn't seem like I was talking forever. And even though cringey is kind of my thing, I had to read the room and understand what was too cringey for each particular group. I also had to learn to walk that fine line between owning my shit and being proud of what I've done and being a braggadocio asshole (I didn't have my hype man to run interference for me).

There was a direct correlation between how much I could make people laugh and how many books they'd buy. Here's the thing though, you can't expect to be 'on' or have a crowd that 'gets' you every single time. Sometimes I just wasn't feeling what I was saying and sometimes the crowd wasn't feeling what I was saying. That's okay, though. I don't need them all to love me. I'm always just looking for my people. I know they're out there, I just have to find them. A lot of times they're hiding. After every single speaking engagement where I'd think, "Hmm, that wasn't so great, was it, Jen?" I'd have someone come and find me. It was almost always a woman.

She'd find me and say, "I almost didn't come, but at the

last minute I decided to pop in. I'm so glad I did, because I really needed to hear that today. I'm struggling and I haven't had a good laugh in a long time and it felt so good. Thank you."

And just like that, all my concerns and worries about not having a terrific event would evaporate.

When I first started putting on pants and getting on planes and going to distant cities to tell my tale and sell my tomes, more than a few of my fellow writers were quite skeptical. "I couldn't do it," one said. "You have no idea what you're walking into."

That's not completely true. Most of the time I knew exactly what I was walking into, because I'd been emailing back and forth with my hostess, I'd pre-sold books, and I knew that most of the people attending actually wanted to be there and knew what they were getting themselves into.

But sometimes, I was going in cold to a group. My reader events were almost always at night, so I asked my virtual assistant to find me other groups I could speak to during the daytime. I'm always looking for women's organizations, book clubs, libraries, civic groups, or whatever she could find.

Those groups were usually the ones I considered "tough crowds." Many of the people in the room had no clue who I was or why I'd been invited and very few did any research on me before I showed up. Sometimes I'd arrive and look around the room and worry they were a waste of my time. That maybe it would have been better to take that free time and get some writing done in the hotel room instead. Lots of times the crowds were mostly male and I find that I don't do as well with men. They tend to find me 'shrill,' 'opinionated', or 'not funny'. Many times the crowds were much smaller than I anticipated and I would think, "Okay, so there's only five people here. It's fine. Give them a good show anyway" and then I'd do my thing.

A few times I had people walk out, but I didn't let them deter me. I just kept going and sure enough by the end, I'd always meet someone who made me feel like I didn't waste one second of my time by being there.

I distinctly remember one group where I had five people show up. When my VA had booked the event, she was told that they always get at least forty-five people, so I was a bit shocked to see only five people sitting there. It was a smaller town and I found out that there was a local parade happening and many of their members were either riding floats in the parade or working at the parade. The five people who had shown up were going to listen to me and then head straight over to the parade too.

I asked if I should give the brief version so they could hurry over and a woman shook her head. "Absolutely not. We want to hear everything you have to say."

So, I did my spiel and when I was done I let them know I'd brought books to sell. That's the thing with these other groups, a lot of times they won't let you pre-sell books, but like I said, if I put on a good talk, I know they'll buy them, so I'm not really worried. But that night I could feel the prickles of doubt creeping in.

Five people, I thought. *How many books can five people buy? Ugh. I won't even cover my dinner tonight.*

But I should have known better. You'd think by now I'd tell my negative brain to STFU because it's always wrong.

The woman who had encouraged me to take my full hour to speak came up to me first. "I don't know if you know, but our group picks one community service project every year to support."

"That's cool. Is it the parade?" I asked.

She shook her head. "No, the parade is just something we do every year. Our project this year is literacy."

I perked up, because I'm all about literacy. Duh. "Oh yeah? That's great."

She continued, "Do you know what Little Free Libraries are?"

"Yes, they're small free libraries around town. It's like a neighborhood book exchange. You can take books or leave books."

"Right. Well, we've built dozens of Little Free Libraries in the neighborhoods in our community. But we just started them and people aren't quite sure how to do it. So we decided that our group would stock the Little Libraries for the first go-round and then we'd encourage our neighbors to trade."

"Good idea," I said, still not catching on.

"I want to buy multiple copies of each of your books as my contribution to the Little Libraries."

OHHHHHHH!!!!! "How many do you want?" I asked.

"I'll take whatever you have."

I don't think she knew what she was saying, because I had a whole box in the car I didn't even bring in with me once I realized only five people had shown up. I don't remember how many I sold to her, but I know I went back to my hotel empty-handed and I could afford room service that night.

All this to say, this is why I never think any opportunity to get in front of people is a waste of time. You never know who is in that audience or what kind of doors in the future they might open for you. The idea that dozens of copies of my books are circulating around that town and being read and shared continually all because one woman decided to go to the parade a little late that night is nothing short of a miracle to me.

How You Can F*cking Do It:

- Get some pants.
- Put them on.
- Say "yes" whenever you can.

17

Don't Forget Why You Do This

"Write hard and clear about what hurts."

Ernest Hemingway

I am in the final stages of getting this book ready for publication so I can push it out into the world and I realized this morning I have one more lesson for you.

I've read and re-read *How I F*cking Did It* dozens of times by now and each time I found myself feeling nostalgic, sad, and even a bit irritated when I was finished. I couldn't understand where these emotions were coming from, so I took a long hard look at myself and tried to figure out what was going on in my head. Why didn't I feel proud or empowered? Why didn't I feel like, "Fuck yeah, we did that, now let's go conquer some more shit, Jen"?

Examining your life can be challenging. Yes, I wrote a lot about my accomplishments, but I also wrote a lot about opportunities I missed or squandered and now I found myself wallowing a bit in the "what ifs." Also, to some it might look like I've done a lot in a short period of time, but you should see the list of goals I set for myself that I never reached (yet). I still haven't done half of what I'd set out to do and that was weighing on me.

But it was more than just professional fulfillment. It was all of it. I'm now in my mid-forties and when I was five years old and dreaming of being an author, this wasn't quite the life I envisioned. It's a lot of hard work and sleepless nights and while I love it, it just isn't quite as romantic and I'd hoped. I'm struggling with aging, too. When I was in my twenties, I heard the loud ticking of my biological clock, but now I feel the cold hands of death closing in on me. I find myself thinking, "I've got twenty-five years, maybe thirty-five if I'm really lucky, to get everything done. To write all the words and get them out there before it's too late." Twenty-five or thirty-five years might sound like a lot to some of you, but the last twenty-five went by in a flash, so I need to get to work!

Yes, I had these fears and doubts creeping in, but that wasn't my real problem. I always have fears and doubts that I'm working through, but for some reason, the last couple of years have been worse than usual and I couldn't figure out why.

And then it hit me.

I'd gotten away from my own rules and my own advice. I'd forgotten what it felt like to just write to vent my soul and ease my inner turmoil. I'd been writing for an audience for so long that I'd stopped writing for myself and I was suffering for it. And it wasn't just me suffering. Everyone around me: my husband, my kids, and even my readers. I'd lost my funny, I'd lost my joy and they could feel it.

When I finally confessed to Ebeneezer how I was

feeling I said, "I think I'm having a mid-life crisis. I'm so unhappy. I'm grateful for what I have, but I want more. I feel like I deserve more. I mean, this can't be all life has to offer. How do I cope with this? Men get sports cars and date twenty-something-year-old women. What do we do?"

"I don't know, but you need to write about it," he said. "I can tell you this, for sure, you are not alone."

He was probably right, but I was still afraid. I was afraid I was the only one who felt that way. I was worried because for the first time since I started writing I was ashamed to write about how I felt. I was worried about hurting the people I care about most with my honesty. I was worried about what strangers would think of me. I was worried about looking like a failure, or worse, a spoiled complainer.

I let the idea of blogging about my mid-life crisis marinate for a few days, I'd been feeling that way for two years, so another couple of days wouldn't hurt.

I woke up in the middle of the night in a panic and I remembered the last time I felt so adrift and unseen, it was when I started my blog People I Want to Punch in the Throat. I'd felt completely alone and kind of crazy. The feelings were back again and I knew what I had to do, there was only one thing that could help me.

I grabbed my laptop and started writing. I didn't think about it or censor myself, I just wrote what was in my heart. It was raw and painful and full of tears. I spit it all out onto the page and within a few hours I hit publish on the blog post called, "Anyone Else Falling Apart Or Is It Just Me?"

The response was absolutely overwhelming. I have no idea how many comments, emails, private messages, text messages, and phone calls I received, but it was a lot. Once again, women from around the world were reaching out to me and telling me their stories. They were thanking me for my "bravery." Little did they know, I wasn't writing because I was brave, I was writing because I'd kept my emotions bottled up inside of me for so long I was afraid I might explode. I had forgotten what it felt like to put my deepest, darkest feelings on paper and then release them into the universe.

One of the emails I received was from a friend who said, "Looks like you're going viral again. That must be a great feeling." I know she was trying to be helpful or whatever, but I didn't write that piece to "go viral." Yes, it hit all the points a viral piece needs to hit and it was clearly resonating with people, but I didn't sit down that night to write hoping I'd write a viral piece again. Like the Elf on the Shelf post, I wrote that Falling Apart piece for me. To chronicle and process my own emotions so I could come out the other side lighter and freer. I'm so grateful that so many people were touched and that maybe I helped them come to terms with their feelings, but to be honest, I wrote that post from a purely selfish standpoint.

Writing that post helped me understand what I've been missing these last couple of years. I've been so focused on building a brand, running a business, and always being "on," that I forgot who I was. I needed that push to get back to my basics. To get back to what I do best, which is to write for my own sanity and to write for others so they know they're not alone. I will try not to forget that again.

How You Can F*cking Do It:

- Remember why you started this journey.

Acknowledgments

Thank you to everyone who has ever read anything I wrote, shared a blog post, subscribed to my newsletter, bought a book, borrowed a book from the library, told a friend about me, put on pants and came to see me, hired me, collaborated with me, friended me, sent a note to me, sent a gift to me, sold a book for me, edited me, designed a cover for me, or just simply laughed at me. You are all my favorites and you are the ones who make this all possible!

A Note From Jen

Thank you for reading this book. I appreciate your support and I hope you enjoyed it. I also hope you will tell a friend—or thirty about this book. Please do me a huge favor and leave me a review anywhere you leave reviews. Of course I prefer 5-star, but I'll take what I can get. If you hated this book, you can skip the review. *Namaste.*

Follow Jen

I hope I've answered all your questions, but I probably forgot some stuff. Feel free to follow me and reach out to me on social media.

Subscribe to my newsletter:
peopleiwanttopunchinthethroat.com

Facebook: Jen Mann, People I Want to Punch in the Throat, I Just Want to Pee Alone, My Lame Life, LadyBalls

Twitter: @throat_punch

Instagram: @piwtpitt

Email: jenmannauthor@gmail.com

Other Books Available

Working with People I Want to Punch in the Throat: Cantankerous Clients, Micromanaging Minions, and Other Supercilious Scourges

People I Want to Punch in the Throat: Competitive Crafters, Drop Off Despots, and Other Suburban Scourges

Spending the Holidays with People I Want to Punch in the Throat: Yuletide Yahoos, Ho-Ho-Humblebraggers, and Other Supercilious Scourges

My Lame Life: Queen of the Misfits

You Do You!
But Did You Die?
I Just Want to Be Perfect
I STILL Just Want to Pee Alone
I Just Want to Be Alone
I Just Want to Pee Alone

Just a Few People I Want to Punch in the Throat (Vols. 1-6)

Made in the USA
San Bernardino, CA
03 June 2019